THE
DOG PAW
Chronicles II

Life Journeys

D. Faye Higbee

With Observations
by Red the Dog

The Dog Paw Chronicles II: Life Journeys

Copyright © 2018 by D. Faye Higbee

All rights reserved. No part of this book may be reproduced, stored in a retrieval system or transmitted in any form or by any means without the written permission of the publisher, except by a reviewer who may quote brief passes in a review or be printed in a newspaper, magazine, or journal.

This is a 2nd edition with numerous updates from the first edition.

Published in the United States of America by
Bitterroot Mountain Publishing House

You may contact the publisher at:
Bitterroot Mountain Publishing House, (bmphmedia.com)
4319 Echo Glenn Lane
Coeur d'Alene, Idaho 83815

Cover photos by Sherrie Jenicek
Interior design by Jera Publishing
Interior photo cover plate by Lawrence McKnight

ISBN 978-1-940025-37-7 (Print)
ISBN 978-1-940025-38-4 (eBook)

DEDICATION

To Red Dog

Red, Leushen, Joshua, Cash, and Faye
(collage by Lawrence McKnight)

FOREWORD

By Josephie Jackson

IMAGINE CATCHING GLIMPSES of your own life reflected through the mirrors of short stories of 'The Dog Paw Chronicles.' It can be startling.

You are both warned and challenged not to find that familiar elements in Faye's stories wrap themselves warmly about you like a friend you had, or didn't, and wanted, when you were oh, so alone and uncertain, or to share the belly laugh joke of yourself.

You will laugh, you will cry, you will listen, and you will remember.

Then, there is Red, the dog.

Red's comments that are faithful and ever loyal, given voice by Faye, I suspect he helped give Faye voice to her own stories. He is the muse, the kind and wise voice we all need. You may be jealous you did not have a Red.

Although the book seems initially 'cute' enough to spike an interest to pick up and read especially with 'opinions' by one's dog during life are included, and even though not all of us are into 'religious,' we can totally understand Faye's (and Red's) spiritual reflection and purpose.

The Dog Paw Chronicles takes you honestly to so many places as if 'in Faye's own head', and bravely (oh, so bravely!), with humor and light grace. You 'listen' with your heart and eyes, much like a child, or

Red, with his face intently gazing into her stories, as he saw them. In the very skillful paring of details, Faye gives invitational space for the reader to insert their own.

Connecting even in the simplest things, like collecting rocks or family misadventures, creates a greater surface area of familiarity that is real and rare.

Like a good bone that tastes better once it has been remembered and sought, found and dug up, earned to be savored now the time is right and the newness mellowed, so Faye's stories and Red's insights in the Dog Paw Chronicles give tugs of invitations to our own, buried and forgotten by busy-ness and avoidance. The sure companions of Faye and Red as they dig up and chew on sometimes serious issues, it is the getting to the marrow of what matters that will have your 'tail wagging' too.

Backed up by Red, Faye will make you braver and kinder to yourself, and for many that is ministry enough.

A dog is happy in their own fur, and so Red encourages Faye in the 'Dog Paw Chronicles' to own her stories, to be content in her own skin and we come along for the journey. Red will firmly put his dog paw print on your heart, but just be careful he doesn't slobber all over you in joy of the ride ... or, is your face wet with tears?

Josephie Jackson

Josephie is a dog lover, author, editor, tea grower, sheep raiser, and many other things. She is CEO on the Bitterroot Publishing Board.

INTRODUCTION

The Dog Paw Chronicles II: Life Journey

THE STARS SPARKLED brightly against the dark blue curtain of the night sky. The tent was warm and cozy with husband Myron and his two friends at the far end. My big black Newfoundland Joshua lay snuggled beside me. Such a calm and peaceful scene. Until all four of them started to snore. ZZZzzzzZZzzZzZZ. So much for sleep THAT night.

My canine pals have traveled this road with me from peak to peak and valley to valley. In their own philosophical way, they have brought comfort and humor into my life. It is only fitting that Red Dog should continue his assistance in my lessons from life, even though he is no longer here.

And besides, if Balaam's donkey can express his opinion, so can Red Dog. Red was a Great Pyrenees/Golden Retriever mix that had more "insight" than other dogs. He seemed to have some sort of special "dispensation" to comment on my life. So he remarked and I wrote. He wasn't very good at typing, so I did that part for him. He was diabetic, not always well, but always faithful and loving. He knew about survival. He knew about sickness, loneliness, abandonment, broken hearts, and anger. He was a rescued pound dog from the Humane Society in Spokane, Washington. And I deeply miss him.

Written in short story form, we will walk through the trials and tribulations of my life together.

I only hope I don't run out of biscuits before the book is finished. My current dog, Cash, would definitely let me know about it.

Faye Higbee

Dogs are more intelligent and insightful than humans give us credit. We have trained Faye in some areas, and are working on her in others. Her first Newfy, Josh, actually forced her to change the television channel once when an occult show was on- he growled and snarled at the TV until she switched it. Smart, huh? We do know what is occurring even in the realms of the spirit. Red Dog

CONTENTS

Section 1   A Miracle Start 1
            1   1953. 3

Section 2   Life Doesn't Come with an Owner's Manual 5
            2   Grandmas R Smart 7
            3   Crocodiles 10
            4   Bullies. 12
            5   Gunpowder 15
            6   Horses. 17
            7   The White Stallions 20
            8   Music 22
            9   Hidden Treasures of the Heart 24
            10   Tina's Tears—The Race Issue 26
            11   Uncle Scotty 29
            12   Blackwatch, Guardian of the Desert 31
            13   Friendship and Orange Juice Cans 36
            14   Death at Christmas 39
            15   Iron Bender 41

Section 3   Europe 1970. 45
            16   The Face of Evil 47
            17   Old Lady in the Hay. 50
            18   Politics 52

19	Blood and Peace............................... 54
20	God and Michelangelo 56
21	Death Camp................................. 58
22	Lipizzaners................................. 60

Section 4	**Adulthood Slogging Through Quicksand** 63
23	Love and Hope...............................65
24	A Girl in a Man's World 67
25	Finding the Stable Pathway 69
26	Marriage Lessons 75
27	PTS and the Voice of Many Waters 77
28	More Broken Dreams 80
29	Fiji the First Time 82
30	Hope Deferred............................... 90

Section 5	**Fresh Horizons** 93
31	Joshua and Mom 95
32	A Keeper................................... 99
33	Wedding Madness 101

Section 6	**Survival Training**............................. 105
34	Mexico 107
35	Waterlogged 113
36	No Cars.................................... 116
37	India...................................... 121
38	Wolves and Warriors 127
39	Soldiers and Full Circles...................... 131
40	A Doctor in the Family 134
41	A River with No Water........................ 137
42	Fiji the Second Time Around 146
43	Goodbye, Dad............................... 153
44	The Call 156
45	Reconciliation 158
46	Farewell to Police Work 160
47	Family Dynamics............................164
48	The Gift 167

Section 7	Bobby Used-to-be Convict	171
	49 Drug Kingpin	173
	50 Brain Bleed	175
	51 Adult Supervision	176
Section 8	Uncle Sam's Misguided Children	179
	52 Curve Ball	181
	53 Tank, Communism Survivor, Marine Veteran, Misguided Child	183
	54 Marines	185
	55 The Ghosts of War	187
Section 9	Cash	191
	56 Proof that we are Dog-Untrainers	193

About the Author 199

SECTION 1
A Miracle Start

CHAPTER 1
1953

THE DOCTOR'S OFFICE reeked of disinfectant. Emma grabbed the cold stainless steel of the counter and pushed herself up to sit on the examination table. She had a feeling the news would be bad. The frown on the doctor's face showed evidence of grief as she delivered the declaration of doom over Emma's pregnancy. There were no miracle drugs. There was nothing they could do. The baby wasn't moving.

The report of possible death echoed in Emma's ears. Eight times previously, death had stolen her babies. She was determined not to experience such despair again.

She took matters into her own hands. She slid off the table, hurriedly dressed herself, raced from the office, and drove in blind desperation to her home just a few short blocks away.

Tears flooded her face. She slammed through the kitchen door and skidded to a stop on her knees under the kitchen table. God would help her now, of that she was certain.

She poured out her heart. "If You will answer, if You will give me a live child, I will give it back to You."

Warmth enveloped her soul. God heard her cry. She knew without a doubt that the baby was alive and well. At that moment, she knew God was real. Death was rejected, as faith took its place.

At the hospital in Spokane, Washington on April 2, 1953, Dorothy Faye was born. Because it was a new procedure for RH factor babies, the surgeons told Emma, "The baby will be a vegetable. You must put it in an institution. The child will probably die before it reaches high school."

Emma ignored them, and with a wave of her hand rejected their prognostications. Sixty some odd years later, I'm glad she did. "God's gift of faith" is the meaning of my name. Emma was my Mom.

God hears every family's heart cries when they want a child. He has a plan for them, and a plan for the child or children He already knows will be theirs. There is a destiny unseen by human eyes that will become reality in the years to come. It only takes one tiny seed of hope.

Red, you are one sharp cookie.

SECTION 2

Life Doesn't Come with an Owner's Manual

CHAPTER 2

Grandmas R Smart

IT WAS 1959, and Grandma's yearly excursion to North Idaho had me and my two Cocker Spaniels perched at the end of the driveway eagerly awaiting her arrival. Grandma was a professional oil painter, a Western artist and contemporary of Charles Russell. Her life encompassed seemingly unending stories about her travels, so I awaited her arrival each summer with anticipation.

Grandma always arrived with a cache of turpentine and oil paints. The smell of turpentine may be awful to some, but for me it meant that she was hard at work, bringing her slide photos to life on the canvas. The fact that I got to sleep on the couch in the living room while she was there was also a sought-after treat. Ok, Grandma also brought presents. Bribes work, when you're talking about Grandkids.

Her red and white dodge station wagon rumbled down the road and parked at her familiar slot in the backyard. I jumped to her aid as she exited the door.

"Grandma! Where did you go this year?" I could hardly wait to hear the stories and see the slides. Grandma always took slides of her journeys. She had been in 49 states and travelled extensively, searching for just the right scenes for her artistry. Adamant about never getting on an airplane, she had driven to all those American places without any qualms whatsoever. I guess she thought that all airplanes were as dangerous as the Hindenburg.

I was enthralled. I wanted to travel too. Something about the freedom of her life appealed to me.

This time, once she had unpacked the car and filled up my bedroom with her luggage and paint supplies, she dragged out a packet of slides. They were shots of a forest fire. She recounted the story about driving slowly through a forest as the flames surrounded her car on both sides. How did she get out of the forest fire? Why didn't her engine blow up? The flames were leaping across the road? She kept me in goose bumps for the whole afternoon. I knew my Grandma was really smart, if she could get out of such a dangerous situation in one piece!

For the rest of the day, she regaled me with stories of riding camels, climbing Pike's Peak, and riding horses on the ranch in Wyoming. She was lucky, Marie Dorothy Dolph, to have experienced so much of life. I longed to experience life like that—with adventure.

Be careful what you wish for.

Finally, it was time for bed. Grandma disappeared into my bedroom. Mom put on the record player for the good night music like she did every night so that I would go to sleep. I fell asleep on the couch to the crooning of Nat King Cole.

A low rumble awakened me. The couch began to slide and shake across the floor. I screamed and jumped out of bed. "Mommy! Daddy! Grandma!"

I sprinted into the hallway. Grandma was already there, her hair standing almost straight up in fear. Or was it that she hadn't brushed her hair. At any rate, she hugged me.

As Mom and Dad crawled out of bed to see what the ruckus was about, Grandma calmly advised them it was an earthquake. Mom and Dad both laughed and insisted we go back to bed. They were convinced we were having nightmares, perhaps from too many home canned dill pickles.

They wandered back to the bedroom and fell asleep. Grandma and I worried that the shaking might not be over. But we eventually fell back asleep, and didn't notice any more shakes, rattles, and rolls.

Morning dawned. The news was brimming with reports of a major earthquake in Yellowstone, Montana. We weren't crazy, after all. Like I said, my Grandma was very smart.

Often memories fade with time, and the good ones can be hidden by bad ones. Grandmothers are often left behind in the struggle to grow up. I've noted that people sometimes push them aside and treat then poorly. Thank goodness, you and your family honored her then and now so that her memory will be alive forever. Although we dogs use smells to figure out what's going on around us, humans catalog them in memories. The memories of your family will always be with you, carefully filed in your heart for times of need.

CHAPTER 3
Crocodiles

"THE RIVER HAS crocodiles in it. Don't play by the water. Be careful." Mom's formidable words echoed through the kitchen. She was using her "mommy voice." While I knew she was fibbing, I chose not go out by the river that day, at least not without my dog Blondie.

It was late in the nippy autumn afternoon. Too cold to play outside, so I played in my room. The dolls were my best friends. We played school with the chalkboard, and I could be the teacher or scientist or whatever my imagination could conjure up.

Someone knocked at the back door. Some friends of Mom and Dad had stopped by for a visit. The parents retired to the basement museum with Mom and Dad. Their teenage boy, however, opened my bedroom door.

He locked the door behind him. Then he grabbed my shoulder and pushed me to the edge of the bed.

"We're gonna do something fun. Sit down." His pants were suddenly unzipped and his private parts were in my face.

I panicked. What is happening? What do I do? It was over in seconds. I felt strangely violated and nauseated.

The boy tried to intimidate me. "Don't tell anyone or else." He sneaked out the door as the family said goodbye.

I immediately ran to tell Daddy who erupted in a loud stream of profanity. Anger rose to his face as he smacked his big hands on the oak table in the kitchen. The smack sounded like thunder to me. He drew me close in a warm Daddy hug.

"Honey this will never happen again. Never. I will not allow it. I will take care of that boy." Dad's face promised, and I knew I could trust him. Since no guns disappeared and no reports of a homicide appeared in the newspaper, I knew that however he handled it, wisdom was the bottom line. The kid never did it again. He grew up to become a good man with a good family.

The situation became a steppingstone instead of a tombstone.

Your parents were right. There are crocodiles.

CHAPTER 4
Bullies

BLONDIE AND I arrived at the bus stop. It was cold out; a skiff of snow covered the country road. We had no shelter, just a tall pine tree that served to keep us from drowning during rain showers. I hugged her and buried my face in her warm fur. She wouldn't keep the bully away, being a sweet little dog, but I felt safe with her. If she was there, I would be ok.

My neighbor swaggered toward me with his brother. Only the oldest boy was a bully. The younger one was a friend. But another fight was inevitable. I could see the smirk on his face. I turned my back in the hopes that ignoring him would stop the problem.

"Your mother is a bitch! I hate her!" The anger in his voice scared me. He shoved me into the neighbor's fence. I swung my Huckleberry Hound Dog lunch pail. Missed. He shoved me again. "Your whole family is a bunch of bitches."

Tears blurred my eyes. The words hurt. I yelled back. Exhaust fumes and a grinding sound interrupted us. The school bus pulled into the road. I heaved a sigh of relief as the bright yellow door swung open.

"What's going on here?" The bus driver's voice was sharp. He frowned as he noticed that my face was red and puffy from crying. He let me on the bus, but stopped the boys behind me.

"You aren't allowed to ride this bus if you're going to push her around. Get your own ride to school." The door shut in the boys' faces. The bully was banned.

I was safe one more time. I needed it to last. No fights again tomorrow, please. He needed to go away. He was several years older than me and not even part of my school. I thought it would be good if he got a car of his own so I'd never have to encounter him again.

At the end of the day the bus dropped me off at the road. Blondie was there waiting in her usual spot. How that dog knew what time it was is beyond me. We walked home together, her presence a soothing touch to the long day. I needed to have Mom and Dad help me with that boy. I couldn't face another day with his mean words. So we had a family meeting over dinner.

Mom handed me a new addition for my lunch pail: a thermos. Dad told me not to let others ruin my life. He promised that bullies are not as strong as they think they are. Bullies lie. Stand up to them. It's ok to fight back. He also mentioned that the kid wasn't a bad sort; he was just going through some problems. But if he didn't listen to the thermos in the lunch pail, he would call the parents.

Morning dawned, and the cycle repeated itself. This time I swung the lunch pail and it connected with a crunch. The boy staggered backwards and ran toward home. The dental appliance in his mouth was broken. Good thing his dad was a dentist. He never shoved me again.

Sometimes bullies have secrets that create their behaviors. Your neighbors were in the midst of a nasty divorce. And, you told me about your parent's divorce at the same time. Both of you had heartaches and couldn't handle them well. Today's bullies are more dangerous than back then, so children need wisdom and good self-esteem to win those battles. They also need to learn how not to listen to the lies that bullies push on their peers. You have to tell them about how that boy grew up. The way it all worked out.

I will, Red, I promise.

CHAPTER 5
Gunpowder

THE SMELL OF gunpowder permeated Dad's boat building shop at the edge of the Spokane River. Earphones dulled the report of gunshots that echoed across the canyon. Loggers, businessmen, federal agents, cops, all filled our home with laughter on Rifle Club night. The guns bucked and roared as the targets ripped from the bullets.

I loved "policing the brass" after they left every week. I vowed to be like them. The thrill of shooting and meeting all the of the law enforcement personnel drew me to that line of work.

One morning after the shooters and their families left, I picked up all the brass and handed the bag to Daddy.

"When can I shoot, Daddy?" I felt ready. At 5 years old I knew I could do it. Never mind that the rifles were bigger than me and my arms would be too short to even hold the thing. Who cared?

I just wanted to be like Daddy and his friends.

Dad smiled. "Soon, honey. When you're old enough. Just remember—you still can't touch any of the guns in the house. It's too dangerous. Death is forever. Guns are for defense only. Never point them at a human unless your life is threatened. Remember that."

I remembered. I also remembered vividly when Daddy torched off a couple of rounds in the air the night someone tried to burglarize his shop at about 2 a.m.. Turned out it was one of Dad's customers who had a tad too much to drink and tried to access his boat after hours. I'm not positive, of course, but I'll bet that guy wet his pants. And the next day he returned to beg Daddy's forgiveness for trying to get into the shop. He never did that again. Yet he still retained my Dad to work on his boats. It was a testimony to Dad's abilities, both as a boat builder and a talker.

The day I turned 9 was a glorious day. Dad gave me my brother's .22 Winchester. Since Dick had gone into the military, then moved to Seattle, he didn't need it anymore. The Hunter Safety Class at school was about to start and now I could participate.

The Coeur d'Alene Rifle and Pistol Club eventually moved to a nicer facility and Dad signed me up right away. There were only a few women in the club, and they were expert shots. I wanted to be like them. I could hear the men brag about their wives' abilities. Others would just remark, "They shoot pretty good for a girl." I was convinced they would say that about me one day.

Dreams and hopes are what drive people to do what they do. It may be something as small as wanting to hear a compliment, it may be something as big as becoming someone important. Whatever the dream becomes, it requires hard work and dedication to achieve.

CHAPTER 6

Horses

FROM THE MOMENT I slid off my brother's rail fence onto Cricket's back, I wanted a horse. The grayish dun Morgan loomed above my head, and she could have squashed me like a bug if she weren't so well trained. My legs stuck straight out over her belly, and with no saddle, her mane was my only hand hold. She simply glanced at me with big brown eyes that seemed to pity my puny size, and lumbered off slowly across the pasture. At the end of the ride, she nuzzled my shirt as if to tell me my novice status as a rider was no big deal. It was an invigorating moment.

Of course, I immediately ran to Dad and asked for my own equine friend. Dad told me that a horse was out of the question, but that our neighbors would allow me to ride "Old Red." We walked up to their barn to meet him, an old sorrel gelding who was the absolute twin to a famous thoroughbred horse named "Man O' War", or "Big Red." I was certain that Old Red was really that famous horse who must have retired to North Idaho … having no clue that they were totally different breeds. Who cares about accuracy when imagination is involved?

As we opened the stall gate, Red stared at me with disdain. *A little kid. Great. Do I need this?* I imagined his reaction. He was an "extra" in the neighbor's pasture, an American Standard that was past his prime, and all he wanted to do was eat. The other horses in the neighbor's stable were Tennessee Walkers, lively horses bred for their beauty and grace. Red didn't care much about grace or beauty; he simply wanted to be left alone. I fell in love with him, stubborn though he was. He readily acquiesced when Dad saddled him, and calmly allowed me sit there without dumping me on the ground. This horse was as large as Cricket, and had a different temperament that made me somewhat nervous. It was a long way to the ground.

Over the next few years, Red's owner, Kit Scates, taught me the basics of horse handling in both English and Western riding styles. We rode together through the woods on trail rides, and galloped or cantered around the riding ring. Red became my project for Horse 4-H, and together we won several ribbons. Once he got used to me, we got along famously. Except perhaps those times he wanted to get back to the barn for some vittles. Then it was "drag the little girl back to the barn" time. I still loved him, and his "crusty" personality endeared itself to my heart.

Of course, there were a few times when he tried to dump me on the ground. On trail rides, he was not thrilled about being last in line, so he would speed up and deliberately trot under the lowest hanging tree branches. I'm pretty sure he would have laughed hysterically if he could have scraped me off his back. Fortunately, I was limber enough back then to bend over flat on the saddle. Today I would likely be stuck and have to be pulled off with a crane.

All in all, I only fell off once, and that was the fault of whoever saddled him for me. The horse bloated his stomach while the cinch was buckled and once in the riding ring, he let all the air out. The saddle slipped sideways and the little girl fell in the dirt. That's ok; I knew how to fall like a sack of wheat. No harm no foul. And at least the horse got a laugh on the human for the day. Horses really do have a sense of humor, if somewhat warped.

Since you are obviously an animal lover of more than just dogs, what else did you have as a child? And did you ever get a horse?

Yes, Red, I had lots of other animals over the years. I had a very mean cat named Tiger that tried to claw his way through life, but Dad got rid of him. A cat flying through the air from the top of the cupboards with all claws out when visitors walked through the front door was not good for business.

Then there were turtles, catfish, guppies, hamsters, parakeets, and finches. The catfish ate the guppies, the turtles and birds froze to death because I left my bedroom window open, and the hamster kept getting loose to poop in my sock drawer. Frankly, I prefer dogs.

As for horses, I did own a lovely sorrel Arabian-Quarter horse mix for a couple of years, but simply could not keep her due to having to farm her out to a neighbor's pasture. I sold her to a young lady who had several horses and loved to ride. Eventually "Wind" became a parade horse of exceptional beauty. Several years later I wandered through the horse barn at our local county fair and found her resting after an exhibition. I do believe she recognized me, as she lifted her head and whinnied, and allowed me to scratch her nose and ears. I cried my eyes out as I petted her. While she was missed, I knew that her life was full and happy. At least if all the ribbons in her stall were any indication. There—you have written proof that I'm a complete marshmallow when it comes to dogs and horses.

CHAPTER 7

The White Stallions

MY BROTHER RICHARD (Dick) was 14 years older than me, so we didn't spend a lot of time together. He was long gone and firmly ensconced in a job in Seattle by the time I was old enough to hold a real conversation.

One winter when I was 10, he stopped by on his way home from a business trip to Hong Kong. He not only brought a present, he offered to take me to a movie. I was ecstatic! It was the premier of Disney's "The Miracle of the White Stallions." It was a horse movie. What could go wrong?

Immediately the sight of the pure white Royal Lipizzaner Stallions dancing and twirling on their hind legs in cadence to music mesmerized me. Their story of redemption from the Nazis during WWII brought a flood of tears through the entire movie. My brother thought I hated it. And my nose was so clogged from crying it was hard to tell him the truth. I loved the movie, no, I loved the horses.

At the moment the movie ended, I set my hope on seeing the horses in person. Little did I know the blessing that waited in my future.

Redemption is important, and not just for horses. Redemption and destiny are demonstrated by the Royal Lipizzans. Their fate rested in the choices of those around them, and because those choices were good, the horses live today as symbols of redemption. Their color at birth is also a symbol of what they become in later life. It's very much like the way people can be black in their hearts, but are redeemed when they get to know God.

You're very smart, Red.

CHAPTER 8
Music

IT WAS RECITAL day at my piano teacher's home. She owned a huge white Victorian house with French doors that gated off the recital area from the rest of the rooms. Behind those doors was the gallery—it was full of parents and kids, all nervously awaiting the announcement of their turn.

Did I practice? Are you kidding? Even at 10 years old, I could play it just fine without too much effort, so I didn't worry about silly things like practice. I had been taking lessons since I was five, so no big deal to me. Expecting my arrogance to cause disaster, Mom was frustrated, and Mrs. Davis awaited my embarrassing mistakes.

I pushed the piano bench back a smidge and sat down at her grand piano. Hayden's Concerto in G was my favorite. My fingers raced across the keyboard. No mistakes (a miracle!). The audience clapped.

Mrs. Davis whispered in my ear. "Your Mom says you only practiced a little. How did you do it? It sounded good. You're a natural. I hope you remember this moment and let music be a part of your life always."

I remembered. I love piano. After 13 years of lessons from Mrs. Davis, I grew to enjoy it even more. I did finally realize that practice was probably important.

Through a few home concerts and playing for political rallies and church worship services, there has never been a moment when piano music did not bring a sense of joy and relaxation to my soul. The moment I start to play, Red Dog runs to the basement family room and lies down at my feet. There is something flattering about that. Dogs love music too.

All creatures can be touched by music. Had you applied yourself it could have become a career. But the fact that music brings such peace and joy to you is a gift both for you and we who love to listen.

Thanks, Red. You were always welcome by the piano, and so is Cash.

CHAPTER 9

Hidden Treasures of the Heart

"DADDY! DADDY! WAIT for me! There are rocks in my shoes and I can't keep up!" I plopped down on a pile of rocks in the Central Oregon desert and waited. I knew Daddy was coming to help me.

"Honey, just empty your shoes." Dad yelled back at me and kept walking.

You're kidding! He's not stopping! I jerked off my shoes and dumped the rocks. Dad had long legs, so I had to hurry to catch up. The desert was hot, rocky, and crawled with a myriad of bugs. I hated bugs. Yellow-jackets, no-see-ums, spiders, scorpions, I hated them all. And ticks, the bane of my existence. Still hate them all today, if truth be told.

We arrived at the digging hole, a deep pit surrounded in boulders and clay. He excavated with a heavy pick deep into the soil. Dad showed me what to look for: ugly clumps of round, brown rocks. They rolled out of the bank right by the bucket as he swung the pick.

He knocked a corner off one of the agates with his rock hammer. Whack! Blues, whites, pinks reds peeked tantalizingly through the edge of the rock as he wet it with his saliva. "No matter how rough it is on the outside, there could be good stuff on the inside," he reminded me. The fear of bugs disappeared in the hunt for treasure. There were so many pretty patterns.

Rockhounds have rocks in their heads, on the kitchen table, in the basement, around the house, and sometimes even in the car. And our basement always smelled like diesel oil which was used to keep the diamond blade from overheating while stones were being cut. Lucky me; my bedroom was directly over the diamond saw, so I got the full force of the odor of diesel. No wonder my clothes always had an interesting smell.

Dad's rubber apron was encrusted with grey and white splotches of grit. He never washed it, so by the time I was in high school it had started to crack from the layer of gunk. When I was very young, he would let me stand under the apron while he cut and polished the gemstones.

I loved to watch as the stone wheels ground away at the rocks. They literally came alive in Dad's hands. Colors arrived at the surface of each stone. Red and gold flowers or a lake with flowers and shrubs around it! Every stone held a hidden treasure. For eons of time that treasure lie hidden deep in the earth, awaiting the process of cut, sand, and polish to reveal its secrets. By the time I grew up I, too, had learned how to find the hidden treasures within stones. It was a practice run for my current life, where I have to dig for the beauty in people.

Sometimes people just keep the rocks in their shoes — all those things that have hurt them over the years. If they would empty their hearts of those painful things, they would have hearts just like those beautiful agates. People and animals are just like those rocks. The outside can be rough, but with a little help, their hearts can change.

CHAPTER 10

Tina's Tears — The Race Issue

THESE DAYS PEOPLE like to say they are non-bigoted, sweet folk who would never, NEVER have a racist bone in their body. I beg to differ. Most of us, whatever color or ethnicity, have some sort of opinion or judgment on others, whether we realize it or not.

My brother and his first wife had three lovely children of their own — Paris, Rachel, and Christopher. They were all blond, blue eyed sweethearts that we knew would have a well rounded education and chance at life. Richard and Jeanette learned of a baby born of both Asian and Black descent who had been placed for adoption by the baby's grandfather without the mother's knowledge. Tina's mom was only 14 years old when she was born. She, too, deserved a life of hope and success. So they adopted Tina.

Tina was a charmer, a cute little cuddly child with sparkly brown eyes and tight curly black hair who could giggle loud enough to wake the dogs in the back yard. The first reaction of my Father and Grandmother to the adoption was total shock. A Black baby? In our family? Oh dear!

Mom, on the other hand, was intrigued and couldn't wait to greet her.

It is a sad to note here that while I truly believed my Grandmother was really smart, she had some sort of glitch in the race area. Her anger towards my brother's decision was vented in a letter soon after the adoption. Tina tells me that she also regularly failed to send her a birthday card while always remembering her siblings.

Dad eventually gave up the horror and embraced the reality. He accepted the adoption and made no further remarks. That doesn't mean he agreed with it, he just kept his mouth shut about it.

Richard's neighbors, on the other hand, were not as easily dissuaded from their foolish feelings. It happened on Easter at the neighborhood candy hunt. All of the candy had been carefully hidden for the neighbor kids. When the time came for scavenging, all of the white children were scooted toward the candy. Tina, on the other hand, was deliberately sent to a corner of the park where no candy was hidden. She found nothing, and wept in total disappointment.

How any human being could deliberately harm another because of the color of their skin was totally beyond our comprehension.

If my brother could have shot the neighbors legally, I'm pretty sure he would have done so. His rage caused them to move from the neighborhood, and eventually send Tina to a private school. As difficult as her beginnings seemed, Tina grew up well. The private school did a much better job of keeping her safe than the public schools. She is deeply loved by all of us, including her brothers and sister. I can only pray that tears over the color of her skin will be few and far between. She's all grown up now, with a husband and grandkids of her own.

Attitudes always surface even in the most innocuous people. There are people who hate whites, people who hate any color except white, and people who just like to hate. It's not always ignorance that produces it, either. Sometimes it's a heart that is shrouded in selfishness and fear. Fear nearly always produces bad behavior. Like people who are afraid of pit bulls. They are the ones who would kill them in a heartbeat. When ignorance and fear (or any other fleshly emotions) run people, bad things happen.

CHAPTER 11

Uncle Scotty

IN EVERY FAMILY there are people who make the hair on the back of your neck stand up. A family can be filled with love and success and yet there will be one standout in every one.

Dad had 3 brothers: Richard, Don, and Scotty. Uncle Don and Uncle Rich were successful businessmen who moved to North Idaho to be with family. Uncle Scotty was the enigma. Born with what was thought to be epilepsy, some of the family shrouded him in shame. His schoolmates made fun of him every day. After all, the Bible said that epilepsy was possession by demons. By the way, that is NOT what the Scripture says — it calls the boy's problem a spirit, and does not say "epilepsy" — Mark 9: 17-27. Never infer things from Scripture. There are medical issues and spiritual ones. Some translations call it "epilepsy", but remember translations often have inferences from the culture in which they are written.

At any rate, some relatives seemed seriously ashamed of Uncle Scotty. So he grew up with no self image — consequently he rarely bathed or cut his hair. The result was a scary-looking man with long greasy hair whom you could smell from a block or two away. He lived on the

Wyoming desert in an old camper and worked as a ranch hand. He had little interaction with the public at large.

In 1979, Grandma passed into eternity at 94 years old. Uncle Scotty drove to North Idaho to attend the memorial service. He didn't know what he was getting in to. While he had come previously with no problems, this time Dad and his brother Rich decided he had to take a bath. No sense emptying the funeral parlor out from the stench, right?

Uncle Scotty was not happy. He fought and yelled and complained as Dad and Uncle Rich literally threw him in the bath tub and scrubbed him down. When the deed was completed, there was a half an inch of red Wyoming mud stuck to the bathtub. It took days to scrape it out. At least he was clean for another decade or so. And he actually presented a decent façade at the funeral. We almost didn't know who he was!

While Uncle Scotty may have looked fierce on the outside, he had a heart of gold. He was a sweet-tempered man who loved to take people for rides in his model T truck for free. Now days he would likely be arrested for being scary, but back then people were excited to ride around the block with him (as long as they held their nose). It was one of my first lessons in not judging a person by their exterior. And it was not the last.

I have noted that humans tend to think that all people who look different must be evil, when in fact, most serial killers look and act like perfectly normal people. Wouldn't it be nice if everyone would wait for their judgments on each other and look deeper than someone's long hair or smell?

CHAPTER 12

Blackwatch, Guardian of the Desert

ONE SUMMER, DAD, Mom and I began a tradition of visiting the high plateaus and deserts of Wyoming in search of nephrite jade. Secrets of majesty awaited me there, particularly in the visage of the wild horse. I had never seen a wild horse, but Dad had shared stories of the herds that once lived near his desert home not far from the Platte River. I had no idea that something wild could affect me. But that summer, a chance encounter changed my heart forever.

Roads across the deserts of central Wyoming in those days were mostly open range sheep or cattle trails. Dad often made his own path in his 50's vintage International pickup. We would thunk and bump across the terrain, occasionally driving in and out of an arroyo. On that first day, a sudden cloud of dust rumbled toward the pickup. Dad slammed on the brakes and leaned toward me. "Watch this, honey, you'll love it."

Out of the dust cloud charged a sleek black stallion, followed by about 15 horses of various sizes and colors. Mom grabbed the camera and snapped a photo. Chestnuts, sorrels, a roan, and even a white horse thundered across the path in front of us. I held my breath as the sound of pounding hooves diminished into the canyon. It was the first contact with a wild horse that I named "Blackwatch," and it wasn't over.

Morning faded into the warm haze of late afternoon. Dad set up camp near an outcropping of rocks just below a ridge. It was safe from flash floods, protected from the wind, and provided a decent base camp for the next couple of days while we explored the desert.

I donned my protective hiking gear, which consisted of a pair of thick, knee-high leather boots. The boots were hot and uncomfortable. It was the rattlesnake factor that required my Dad to exercise his parental right to make me wear them. He had been bitten as a child, so boot protection against snakes was mandatory in our family. I'm pretty certain that any rattlesnake that tried to bite me through those boots would have broken a fang or two. Fortunately, we never had to test the theory. In all the years of clambering up steep rock piles like a mountain goat, I never so much as heard a rattle.

We left Mom to prepare dinner, and trekked off across the landscape to reconnoiter the direction we'd take in the morning. By the time we returned to camp, my feet hurt, and all I wanted to do was sit in the camper door and watch the wildlife.

As the light started to fade, a small herd of pronghorn antelope took up residence near the camper. They didn't seem to be intimidated by our presence. I watched them quietly, enjoying their graceful beauty. Suddenly a glimpse of black snagged my attention. It was that black stallion, the alpha leader of the wild horse herd we had seen earlier.

Dad saw him too. As excited as I was to be that close, Dad put his hand on my shoulder and admonished me not to push it. "Honey, those hooves are very sharp. And he is wild, even though he's close. If you scare him, he'll run, but if you get too close and make him feel threatened, he can hurt you very badly."

I heeded his warning, but everything inside me wanted to run to the horse and throw my arms around his neck. He was beautiful. Even in the fading sunlight, his raven black color seemed to shine with bluish luster. He stood like a sentinel very close to the camper on a short rise. Behind him there were muffled whinnies and flickers of tails. His harem was close.

I carefully edged around the camper door until I had a clear line of sight and began to sing softly. Instantly the impossible happened: the stallion and I made eye contact. Our gazes locked, and in one fleeting moment an unfathomable bond occurred.

He pawed the ground, nodded his head up and down, and his mane tousled over his face. Was it a sign of acceptance? Or was it a warning? I didn't know, so I kept singing.

The antelope gradually returned to foraging, and moved off around the rocks. I remained frozen as if in a sort of time warp, staring at my horse and longing for him to talk to me about his herd. Blackwatch remained in his place, a guardian of strength and power. Unknown dangers surrounded him, yet he steadfastly held his ground, the perfect picture of a leader who protected his family without hesitation. He was now my horse, my friend. I could never own him, yet it seemed as though he belonged to me alone. He was the black stallion of my dreams.

Dusk descended and the horses vanished into the night. But they didn't vanish from my heart. Summers came and went as I grew into my teens. We frequented the Wyoming deserts every year, and every year, Blackwatch and the herd raced across our path on the way to the campsite. That he was able to maintain his position as leader was an admirable trait. It meant that he was as wise and powerful as he appeared. I looked forward to our meetings, our quiet moments of watching each other by the outcroppings. And he always responded to my soft singing with that familiar nod of his majestic head, and a pawing of hooves in the dirt. Often I would forego the jade expedition for a couple of hours, and sit quietly watching Blackwatch guard his herd.

But then, one summer, Blackwatch did not cross our path. Neither did any herds of wild horses. The sand was void of hoof prints, and no dust clouds obscured the horizon. My friend, my guardian of the desert was gone.

In a child's heart dwell stories, hopes and dreams for tomorrow. Blackwatch had been a story of friendship, a love of wild creatures, a symbol of freedom, a leader whose spirit seemed to call to me. His constant presence on our rock hunts gave me a strange sense of security. He exhibited an alluring strength, a spirit that had captured my heart and imagination forever. I had no idea where he went, and my heart was completely broken. Dad asked around his desert-dwelling friends, and the news came: the herd had been rounded up by the government, its fate unknown.

I didn't really want to know, if truth be told. But stories of slaughter and torture of wild horses reached my ears anyway. The 1971 Federal law to establish reservations for the wild horse allowed the Bureau of Land Management the right to round up any excess horses from public lands and put them up for adoption. While they vehemently denied any slaughter, the fact was that the magnificent horses were no longer safe and free. Even the thought of my friend's herd being split apart and confined as pets broke my heart. If Blackwatch had been placed for adoption, I could not find him; he had disappeared from the landscape entirely. I was inconsolable.

As the years went by, I wondered about the wild ones and what might have become of them. In 1992, on a rock hunt to Nevada, I asked my husband Myron to stop at the Palomino Valley National Wild Horse Adoption Center just north of Sparks, Nevada. I wanted to see for myself the conditions of their lives.

What greeted me crushed me. In the corral closest to the road, several mustangs stood jammed in together nose to tail. They were scraggly, unkempt, sad creatures whose spirit had been broken by mere placement in confinement. I saw the sorrow in their eyes, and felt the loss of freedom in their equine hearts. And I couldn't handle the grief. My husband, with great sympathy, told me that our rock hunt would be on the Black Rock Desert, and we were sure to see wild horses living free. My heart yearned for it to be true.

We turned off into the desert at Gearlock, Nevada, an inhospitable place of volcanic rock and intense heat. Summer temperatures often stay over a hundred degrees for long periods of time. We drove off into the wilderness, careful not to go too fast, lest the volcanic glass called obsidian pierce our tires. It wouldn't do to be stranded in such a dangerous environment.

As we bumped along the rocky paths, we rounded a short rise and came upon two wild horses. Two sorrel mustangs warily watched our progress. The mare was bedded down at the edge of a short ridge in what shade she could garner. She was obviously pregnant. The other horse, a stallion, stood guard over her. Once again, a guardian of the desert stood watch over his charge. Though I loved to see those beautiful horses wild and free, the vision of Blackwatch haunted me. I saw no black wild horses that day. My friend had faded into history, my history, a place that only my heart would keep.

Will people ever understand the importance of protection for their nations, their families, or even the planet? Blackwatch was a sentinel. People should learn from the wild horses instead of destroy them. I know this isn't the end of the story about Blackwatch. Don't forget to tell them.

I won't, Red.

CHAPTER 13
Friendship and Orange Juice Cans

I REMEMBER THE EXACT day when I realized how important friendship was. It was the day that my BFF Shirley got married and moved away. (BFF—Best Friend Forever). How two people so wondrously opposite could become friends was an absolute miracle. She lived in the city, her Dad was a Democrat, and she didn't care for guns. I lived in the country, had guns in every corner of the house, and both parents were diehard Republicans. And yet, we were nearly inseparable. And our moms got along famously.

We attended the same church, a Community Presbyterian-Methodist mixture that had been in our home town of Post Falls, Idaho for nearly a century. We sang in the choir together, fully believing that God was an alien from outer space. Probably a good thing that the church leadership was clueless on that point.

Growing up in the late 60's it was important to have straight hair. Shirley and I had, well, let's just call it "naturally unruly" hair. So in order to be "cool," we set our hair on orange juice cans and used very stinky chemicals on it to try to get that straight "Twiggy" look.

No success. Shirley ended up with smoother kinks; I ended up with damaged frizzy hair. It took years before the real curls revealed themselves. I guess my hair was waiting for a time in history when Albert Einstein hair was ok.

We picked wildflowers together and made a science project out of it. (Got an A, by the way). We went with Dad on rock hunting trips and ended up covered in dirt from head to toe. Her poor Mom would simply smile, shake the clothes out, and throw them in the washer. Her mom and my mom: women who had the patience of Job.

We both spent hours and hours at the library, and dragged home stacks of books to read. We were champion debaters, with many trophies to our names. How can two people of diverse backgrounds do that? We had true friendship. And friendship covers a multitude of backgrounds.

Music was in our blood. She played the piano for my saxophone solos in school, and I played the piano for her flute solos. We played in marching band, pep band, and anything else we could involve ourselves in. We even participated in school plays. We were busy kids. No grass grew under our feet.

Both of us helped with political campaigns. I mean, both of us helped <u>both</u> parties. We stuffed envelopes and shoved them in mailboxes. We played the piano for their functions. We knew there were differences, but it seemed like the right thing to do, considering our parents were on different sides of the spectrum. Today, we are both more alike than different, a product of our experiences in life.

While my Grandma was an accomplished artist, I could only draw stick people with any degree of ability. Shirley, on the other hand, could draw all sorts of things. Today she, like Michelangelo, can find grand shapes and beauty in a lump of clay. My cupboards are filled with her lovely pottery pieces. I wouldn't have it any other way.

While I had many wonderful friends in High School and still love them today, Shirley will always be a BFF. And at 60 years and counting, I am grateful for every single moment.

It seems like humans are less prone to opinions when they're young. It would be better if people would keep a little childlike attitude when they grow up. True friendships are timeless and last over long distances. People don't realize the importance of true friendships. If they understood the value of relationships, their politics would not be as filled with angst.

I think you should speak to the Congress, Red.

CHAPTER 14

Death at Christmas

IT WAS AN extremely cold Christmas. Ice and snow blanketed the ground around the house, and the Spokane River was frozen all the way across. The entire Dolph family descended on our home for the Holidays. As the last minute Christmas Eve shopping was completed, we all expectantly awaited the morning and the tearing of wrapping paper. The presents were piled almost to the top of the Christmas tree in the living room, which created an impossible sleep situation for us kids.

By Christmas Day, most of the family had gathered in the kitchen to play cards after the mess we kids created in the morning. Uncle Richard knocked on the back door. But the time I got there to let him in, his face was as white as a ghost. He stepped into the house and turned around to stare at Rex, our new puppy, who was wagging his entire body on the back stoop. Uncle turned to us and swore that Rex had greeted him in English.

"He said 'Hi, Rich'," my Uncle stated flatly. "I heard him say it. Your dog is very scary." With that pronouncement, he sauntered in to the kitchen for a drink.

Rex was a Husky-Norwegian Elkhound mix. His fuzzy fur was a mixture of brown, silver, and grey. At only 10 months old, we knew that he would grow up into a powerful addition to the family.

Grandma and most of the adults began their Canasta game. I moseyed over to help Mom cook dinner.

Screaming abruptly interrupted the family get-together. Dad jumped out of his chair and was out the door in a flash. We all crowded around the window in time to see one of my cousins, Chucky, weeping uncontrollably, walking toward the house from the River. Dad was wet and carrying the lifeless body of my dog.

My throat constricted. I couldn't breathe. My dog was dead.

Dad came in the house a few minutes later. He grabbed me and hugged me tight. Mom was crying too. Chucky had tried to play fetch and the piece of bark skittered onto the ice. Rex went for it and broke through. It was too late to save him. My baby was gone. My Christmas was ruined. I ran to the bedroom to cry. I knew it wasn't Chucky's fault, but I wanted to blame him. My heart was thoroughly crushed. The presents didn't matter anymore. Death had stalked my Christmas.

Did you forgive Chucky? Sadness can sometimes produce bitterness that hangs on for years.

Yes, Red, I forgave Chucky.

CHAPTER 15
Iron Bender

HOWARD DOLPH WAS a builder of steel boats. Many of the tugboats that once serviced the Forest Industry's moving of logs in North Idaho, along the Columbia River, and Lake Roosevelt in Washington were created by my Dad. Like the Michelangelo of metal, he took sheets of steel and bent them to his will. He always referred to himself as an "Iron Bender."

Every new tug boat had a personality. The Pine Cat, Slushy, Florence Lee, many others, all had fun names, and all could tow thousands of board feet of logs through the river systems. They were all referred to as "she." I would say they were the ultimate in "working women."

One time I asked to steer the Pine Cat. I learned that while the men all thought they steered easily, my puny little muscles weren't quite up to the task. The thick steel cables attached to the steering column were made for big dudes, not cheeky little girls.

As time passed, Dad developed a dream. He sought a different type of boat on Lake Coeur d'Alene. In the early 1900's steam ships once criss-crossed the lake, ferrying tourists from all over the Northwest.

The only cruise boat left in the early 1960's was a dance barge pushed by another boat. In his imagination, he planned a self-propelled cruise boat with a nice dance floor and bar. He envisioned the lake would once again be home to special cruises that would draw more tourists to its scenic shoreline.

In between tugboat jobs, the new boat took shape in the shipyard at our home. Sheets of steel beaten and heated, boards of wood bent and nailed, two fluted smokestacks — and the Mish-an-nock was born. The name meant "Morning Star", a Kalispel Indian name chosen by our Campfire girls group.

Launch date July 18, 1968 showed up in gale force winds and a nasty rain storm. The "Mish" was painted a lovely white with red trim, 65 feet long with a handmade agate bar. Like a woman all dolled up for a debutant ball, she was ready for her moment of fame. It was only raining sideways, so we weren't at all concerned enough to cancel the event.

The news media arrived with TV cameras. Miss Idaho was resplendent with her glittering crown and white formal gloves. She just lived across the river from us, so we were hopeful that she wouldn't drown getting home after the ceremony. A local resort owner, Robert Templin, arrived with the christening champagne. The cruise boat would be christened with the best!

Dad tied the bottle to the h-bit, where the ropes tied the boat to the dock. Miss Idaho swung the bottle of champagne hard at the bow of the boat. Nothing happened. It bounced off the bow and hung there, dejectedly swinging in the wind. The bottle was too thick to break, even against the steel bow! They uncorked it, poured it into glasses, poured one over the front of the boat, and toasted to her success. At that point, the Mish-an-nock slipped slowly into the River. Dad's dream was only the beginning for Lake Coeur d'Alene.

The Mish-an-nock ushered in a new phase of our lives. Dad juggled the captain's position, and Mom had to learn how to be a bartender. He let me steer her into the moorage slip once, and it was a great wake-up call on paying attention to details. One wrong move with twin Caterpillar engines and the entire public dock system would have been destroyed. I did it just fine, but decided that the whole "boat captain" thing was better handled by someone who wouldn't clench their teeth so hard.

People from nearly every walk of life patronized the cruises—from an Idaho governor to visiting tourists from overseas. Even locals enjoyed the scenic trips. Our senior class "sneak" day was held on the boat, as a handful of adventurous souls from my Post Falls high school class skipped school to take a boat ride. (Shhhh, don't tell anyone).

When I reached 18 and could legally be a waitress, I quickly learned that trying to take drink orders from drunk people was not my calling either. I didn't know a gin and tonic from a Harvey Wallbanger.

Over the years the Mish-an-nock served thousands of tourists on lake journeys, and occasionally rescued a private boat or two from storms. Today it has been refurbished and still sails the coastline of Lake Coeur d'Alene with passengers from all over the world.

By the mid-1970's, Mom and Dad were both exhausted. He sold the Mish to a local resort owner, moved to Oregon, divorced Mom one final time, and remarried. (Oh, yes, in case you were wondering, they were divorced and remarried several times. Nobody said they didn't love each other.) In spite of the stresses, Dad always made sure we were well cared for. While we weren't wealthy, and I missed out on a couple of scholarships because of our income being on the dividing line, Dad never left me to dangle like that bottle of champagne.

Lots of humans don't have a good father. You can relate to God easier than some, because you had a father that would provide for his family no matter what. Just like God. And your Dad left a legacy, part of the history of North Idaho. You can be proud of him for sure.

I am, Red. Very proud of my Dad.

SECTION 3
Europe 1970

CHAPTER 16

The Face of Evil

IN A MARVELOUS turn of circumstances, several students in my high school class were invited to take a trip to Europe in the summer of 1970. It promised to be a huge adventure! After a round of staying with families in England, we crossed the English Channel and headed by bus toward Communist Europe.

We had heard the stories of the Cold War. And there we were, stopped at the border of Hungary, awaiting clearance to enter. We felt like we were stuck in a spy movie and could hardly wait to see what happened next.

There was a guard tower at the crossing point, the guards all carried machine guns, German Shepherds trotted beside the guards. Signs warned of land mines. Barbed wire and searchlights stretched through the forest and along the Danube River. The stories were true. Their citizens were trapped. No pictures were allowed in military areas. I scrunched down in the seat, hoping to see what I wasn't supposed to see. I peeked above the edge of the window. Darn. There was no time to snoop.

The bus door slid open; the guard stepped inside.

"All passports." His voice was terse, no emotion. Fear engulfed all of us.

His brown hair was greasy, slicked back under the military hat. He took my passport and sarcastically laughed at my photo. So I dressed up for it, so what? The guy was a jerk.

He flipped through the pages and his eyes narrowed.

"Visa is for Gorican. Not for Hungary. All passports here. Now! Be quiet." He fingered the grip on his gun and reached out to confiscate all passports on the bus. We were trapped just like them.

We drove to the hotel in Budapest. The clouds were dark and foreboding. The gray weather made the city look dreary. The air smelled like diesel or burning coal. The people wore drab colors and didn't smile much. Dilapidated roofs, chipped paint, the buildings seemed forgotten somewhere in the movie. Not many cars, a few trucks overloaded with hay. The people seemed sad. They didn't look us in the eye. Their expressions were … like trapped animals, hunted. They felt hunted — pursued by their government.

Our group met in the lobby of the hotel. We prayed together and talked through our fear in a democratic demonstration in full view of the hotel staff. The bell hops, the cleaning personnel, all watched us from the hallways. They were curious at the Americans who could voice their opinions on anything and pray in public. But we were afraid and wondered: Would the Communists let us go?

Government shouldn't try to control people. The more governments try to force people to obey, the more damage is done to their citizens. It's like people who abuse their children or animals — they beat them, yell at them, tell their kids they are worthless, or use spike collars on dogs or spurs on horses. It can be fixed, but it's a hard, long road.

Red, I nominate you for President.

CHAPTER 17

Old Lady in the Hay

THE HUNGARIAN TOUR guide spoke in abrupt, unyielding words. No pictures of soldiers. No pictures of government places. No. No. No. No walks by yourself. No noise. I wondered if anyone could do anything in Hungary.

Russian soldiers were deployed loosely everywhere. An uprising in Czechoslovakia had the Kremlin nervous, so they had deployed thousands of troops in nearby countries. Blue uniforms with red collars on every corner. I carefully hid behind my classmates so that I could take photos in spite of her warning. They didn't show much, but it felt like I had defied the Communists and won. (That curiosity thing again).

The bus threaded through narrow streets to a Cathedral. It sported a mosaic roof of kaleidoscopic colors and patterns. Blue, red, yellow, real gold on the edges. There was a statue of St Stephen, King of Hungary, astride a horse in front. The entire building was an amazing feat of artistry.

The tour guide pushed open the huge wooden doors. She was quite proud, but not of the cathedral, of what the Communists had done.

"This was once a place of myths. But we use it for more practical things. We now have cattle here." She pointed arrogantly to the once mighty sanctuary. Hay and cows. Stalls where pews once stood. No lights, no Bibles, no choir music. Darkness and the smell of cow manure. I wanted to yell at her, but held my tongue.

A glimpse of light caught the corner of my eye. I dropped back from the group and peered into a stall. It was an old lady on her knees in the hay. A tiny flickering votive candle lit the floor in front of her. The babushka covering her hair was grey like the Hungarian sky, and her faded, tattered clothes hinted of a dark blue. Her holy wool socks were rolled around her calves. She was praying. Her lips moved in silence as in her peasant way she defied the government. The flame danced with life, throwing shadows against the dark stall. She was nothing to them. She was no threat, so they let her be. An old woman in the hay.

If the Communists had known about the power of prayer, they would have stopped her. An old woman was the biggest threat of all.

By the way, Red, with the fall of the Iron Curtain that cathedral once again has services. You are correct—that woman's prayers were mighty!

CHAPTER 18
Politics

THE NEXT DAY we were off to the Young Pioneer Camp, the training camp of Communist Youth. We were stringently warned: "be quiet, don't start fights. You are Ambassadors for America. Use self-control." The leaders were quite firm about it.

But I wanted answers. They all looked alike! They had dark pants, white shirts, red ties. And they were not Campfire kids. They were removed from their parents at an early age to be indoctrinated by the Communists. After all, their parents couldn't be trusted with raising their own children. They might become suspicious of communism or something else insidious.

There was no TV from America, so they didn't hear the 'real' news. The government heavily controlled the news media, and no outside influences were allowed. They were steeped in propaganda. "America is evil." "America is trying to conquer the world." "America started the Vietnam War." I knew I could fix them if given a chance.

The building was stark, meagerly furnished, and had a cold, unfriendly atmosphere. I decided to tell them the truth. One boy yelled at me in Hungarian. Didn't understand a word he said. We balled up our fists and started shouting at each other. I knew I would win. I'd show him. I'd make him understand. Unfortunately for me, he wasn't interested in my American viewpoint. Just as we locked into the fight mode, the teachers pulled us apart.

I had violated international protocol and received a short lecture. "We told you not to start fights. They can't understand because they are taught different. Leave it alone!"

I still knew I was right, of course.

Opinions are like trees planted as seedlings. They grow in soil that is fertilized by the environment. The longer the seedling remains in that soil, the harder it will be to uproot it later. Changing the opinions of others is a process. It's like training an aggressive dog. You can do it, but it will take patience and discipline.

Red, would you like to be a delegate at the UN?

CHAPTER 19

Blood and Peace

HUNGRY LIONS. LOUD screams of agony. Shredded flesh. Spurts of blood. Metal on metal clashes. The clank of armor and sword. The Coliseum in Rome. The place of blood. The sport of murder. The uproar of the crowds. My imagination took flight at the Roman tour guide's words.

I grasped the stone railing as nausea struck. The history of death screamed into my soul. How could civilized people let this happen? How could hatred become a sport? I stared at the floor of the Coliseum and tried to blot out its vicious history. The images would not leave. I became uncomfortable with Rome at that moment. The rest of the Roman countryside and ruins left me with nothing but a love of history. This was different.

We moved on to the next stop; the catacombs under the city. Mildly claustrophobic, I dreaded the whole prospect.

The chambers were carved out of solid rock. Oddly, I felt completely safe in the tunnels. It wasn't dark. It should have been dark. The caverns should have been dank, but they were dry. We walked further through the tunnels. Underground, no lights. Ancient worship place.

Were angels there? My mind raced. Oil lamps. Candles. Quiet. Chapels of stone. Places where Believers met with God. Tombs with pictures of the brethren lined the walls. Carved with love and honor of the fallen. Safety. Eternal resting place. I felt completely at peace under the streets of Rome.

Peace comes in a place of worship. Like when you worship on the piano, the sounds soak into the atmosphere. Their worship soaked into the stones of the catacombs, whereas the blood of victims from the Coliseum cries out from the ground above. The earth itself remembers. If only mankind would understand that what they do has repercussions far beyond the moment.

CHAPTER 20
God and Michelangelo

AS MUCH AS my imagination tried to hold me hostage in some spots, the art in Italy was a treasure to behold. Italy is home to exquisite statues in nearly every city, with a rich, deep history of reverence toward God.

Florence had King David. I wondered if he really looked like that, as Scripture mentioned something about him being skinny. I was certain that the church ladies would faint if I showed them any photos. A buck naked king with perfect, strong muscles—I snickered at the thought of their reaction. His face reflected peace and gentle strength, so I hoped they would look beyond the statue itself.

Michelangelo was a sculptor who could reveal a powerful man inside of a block of stone. He had an important gift. Take nothing and make something grand. I hoped that I would one day find my gift. Make something grand out of something lifeless... I wondered.

The Pieta testified of a mother's grief. It was literally etched into Mary's face. Intense. Inconsolable.

The entrance to the Vatican had massive carved wooden doors that swung open like a castle. It was dark inside, with light rays that streamed through the windows. Statues invaded nearly every corner!

One alcove featured Moses. His frown was etched in stone forever, a reminder of the people's sins. Michelangelo brought him alive, chiseled with perfection in dark mottled marble as he sat on the stone pedestal. He had become God's chosen once again. He clasped the Commandments close to his side. Such love in the stone. Such truth in the subjects; it was breathtaking.

The Sistine Chapel held dizzying scenes of eternity painted on the ceiling of the church. Angels, The Saints surrounded us. I twirled in a circle and grabbed a shoulder of my friend Marcia to steady myself. God the Father touched Adam the beginning. Life flowed from One to the other. Not like lightning, more of a connection.

Michelangelo connected. His art touched heaven. David's strength, Moses' power, the Pieta's agony, Michelangelo was passionate for the heart of God. That's why there was life in his art. There was life in the connection. We need connection too. Life exists where there is connection to God.

Connection, relationship is one of the most important concepts of life itself. Connection to God, connection to each other, it is the foundation of civilization's hope for the future.

CHAPTER 21

Death Camp

DACHAU, GERMANY, WAS an infamous Death Camp. Slumps in the earth extended across the compound in rows, blanketed with tiny red flowers that rippled in the breeze. They were reminders of innocent blood.

The pictures on the memorial frightened me. The tour guide pointed to the photos and told us some Nazis thought it was fun to shoot the people; shove them into the pit. "They're not people, just animals."

We shuffled slowly along the row of gas chambers. Typhus and lice, disease and starvation. People pushed inside for a "shower." The door locked behind them. Gas flowed. Death sucked the oxygen out of their lungs. Breath was ripped from them. Bodies to the incinerators. More bodies piled on the ground. Bodies in the boxcars. I couldn't listen anymore.

I stared at the remains of a prison built with hate. It almost caused me to faint. They were human beings. Not worthy of death. Worthy of love. Blackness enveloped me; I had to get out of there. I ran back to the bus.

Never again, I thought. Hatred will not win. We will remember. I remember.

"I never hate. Hatred only brings more hatred." Alice Herz-Sommer, the oldest living Holocaust survivor, quotation from **"Alice Dancing Under the Gallows,"** 2010.

CHAPTER 22
Lipizzaners

HIS WOBBLY LEGS only held him up long enough to sway for a minute and then buckle. He fought his way back up on the narrow spindles. A black foal, freshly born, still wet from his mother's birth canal. He was the tiniest package of miracle I had ever seen.

The little creature stumbled around his stall like a drunken sailor for several minutes until he finally got his "sea legs." This funny little horse would one day bring audiences to their feet as he danced around an arena on his back legs. His black countenance would be transformed into white perfection, as the shaky past fell away into choreographed destiny. How fitting it was to see destiny play out in the Royal Lipizzan stallions. From the tears shed in a movie to tears shed in the stable in Vienna, that birth was a true miracle of redemption and destiny that I will never forget.

Destiny is often created by miracles. By God's hand the Lipizzan stallions were saved from annihilation. God saved your life, you saved my life. Our lives connect on a level far beyond what our eyes see. We don't know, as we traverse this life, what lies beyond our present circumstances. But we are all destined for a purpose, whether to dance or to write. I hope that all the readers will find their portion of that destiny.

Me, too, Red. May all of them find their portion.

SECTION 4

Adulthood Slogging Through Quicksand

CHAPTER 23

Love and Hope

THE JAIL STANK of dirty socks and urine. How could they work there? The office was cluttered, with papers lying around in piles. Garbage cans were overflowing. Did anyone ever file anything? I wondered. I caught myself. I should shut up and mind my own business.

I glanced around their office, looking surreptitiously for my favorite handsome deputy. He was nowhere to be found. Obviously he was not on duty that day. I dropped off the paperwork and started to leave.

Almost out the door, I caught a glimpse of the bulletin board. A picture was stuck there with pins. I squinted in the dim light. It was a picture of me. They had posted a news article about me! A circle had been drawn around my face with a remark beside it. "Eagle beak." It was my "friend's" handwriting.

The tears were instant. I ran for the door. Why did he do it? I was devastated.

I sprinted to the car. My vision was blurred, couldn't see the road. It felt as though my life was over. Pain ripped through my chest. I couldn't face tomorrow or even today. First my roommate went bad; then the guy who seemed to like me turned out to be a phony. It was time to end my life.

I called Mom and Dad, but they were fighting that day, so weren't interested in their drama queen daughter's problems. I called some of their friends. They weren't interested in hearing my broken heart either. They were too busy. They said I could come over tomorrow. Maybe. No one had time for me. Life wasn't worth living.

Still desperate, I called the psychologist from college Psych class. He invited me over. Don and Julie Sprague were caretakers of a lovely white Mansion by the lake. I pulled in the driveway and walked through the icy back lot to the door.

Julie had filled the tea pot for us. Don opened the French doors to the parlor. The sun radiated warm through the glass. Scattered poinsettias around the room brought a cheery Christmas feel to the house. The ancient oak floors squeaked as I stepped into the room. It felt like a safe place.

We talked. I talked. They listened. I listened. Hours passed. Suddenly, I felt lighter. Don's words soothed my heart. They are words that will never be forgotten.

"Never be afraid to love." He said, "Sometimes it hurts. Too many people in the world can't love. You are one who can. You are special."

Love isn't real when it's one-sided. If only all humans would understand how important hope is and how to give it away to everyone. Whether it's a lonely animal left at a shelter or a person with a broken heart, all are in need of hope. False hope can bring more destruction, so it must be real, backed by love and truth.

CHAPTER 24
A Girl in a Man's World

IN 1973 I was hired full time at the local police department. My former nemesis from the neighborhood already worked there, and when we saw each other he didn't even make a snide remark. He had long since grown past his bully days after a stint in the US Army. He seemed almost nice considering our turbulent past. Eventually, he even became my boss, the Chief of Police. We got along famously. Of course it may be that he thought I still had that metal lunch pail. Yet he was one of the few that seemed to have no personal grudge against women.

One day in the early years, I asked to go to recertification training for my emergency medical card. The Captain emphatically stated no. "You can't go to the school for medical recertification. You're a girl."

The answer was so directly nasty that I was temporarily stunned. I tried to request a reason why, but was totally ignored. So I started job hunting. That was an exercise in futility. In the early 70's, the beginnings of the Women's Rights Movement had brought bitterness and anger to the issues surrounding equality. After a short time in NOW (National Organization of Women), I decided that they, too, had succumbed to bitterness and anger and I wanted no part of it. So I continued my search for work.

Several interviews later, after having been told by many different agencies that "girls would get pregnant and quit their jobs," I gave up and stayed put. At least it was a paycheck. And eating and living indoors was pretty important.

One afternoon, the law enforcement shooting competition was in full swing. It was snowing out, not a finger-friendly day for shooting unless you could do it in gloves. I had a 30-06 and wanted to shoot with the men. The women had a hissy fit.

"You can't shoot with our husbands," they whined. The husbands said yes she can. The fight was short, but I bet some of those men slept in the doghouse that night. They let me into the rifle competition. I had never shot a rifle larger in caliber than a .22, and knew it would kick hard, so I held it close to my shoulder. Big help.

Boom! Boom! Boom! All the weapons fired at once — a huge explosion of sound. My body vibrated. My ears rang even through the earphones. Boom! My shoulder hurt. Boom! Only a few more shots. Boom! Boom! Finished.

They checked the targets. Not too bad. Not perfect. The men stared at me. I finished third, with bruises. Pretty good for a girl, they remarked. It felt good to finally hear it.

One milestone reached, many more ahead. Always remember to keep going and not camp out at the place where that milestone was reached. I am hopeful that you forgave the lot of them for their failure to understand the worth of women.

Yes, Red, I forgave them.

CHAPTER 25

Finding the Stable Pathway

IN THE EARLY years, as female multi-tasking employees, we did everything: statistics, filing, report writing, phones and front desk, dispatching, writing parking tickets and frisking female prisoners. There were no "regular" female officers at that time, just we who were considered "Class C" officers. We were certified, but only allowed to function in certain areas.

My very first call as a dispatcher was intense. A man was choking to death at the local VFW hall. The caller had no idea what to do. He wasn't breathing. I remained calm and walked her through the procedure for choking and CPR. She cleared his airway and started the procedure. The ambulance arrived at the scene within minutes. The man survived and the woman was ecstatic to be able to save a life.

It was the cold turkey method of dispatching, thrust into a life or death situation with only book-learning to get me through. Within a short span of time it became easier. At least if the officers stopped harassing me. From spraying my microphone with MACE to putting a frog on my desk, life was a never-ending challenge in those days. Ok, so it never stopped being a challenge. But at least the men stopped picking on me at some point. Sigh.

Desk duty was not always my favorite position. You never knew who would enter the department—friend or foe. One day a man entered the door with a puffy red face: obviously enraged.

"My car was stolen. It's a Volkswagen."

I pulled out the papers started to fill out the state-required report. I wondered—why would anyone steal a yellow Volkswagen Bug in winter? It was snowy outside, and I figured whoever stole the car was not from North Idaho.

The phone rang. Deann, the dispatcher on duty, hollered from the radio room. "Hey, is that VW a yellow one?"

I nodded. DeAnn started laughing. She choked up with tears running down her face and could hardly talk. The lady on the phone thought that someone was following her in a yellow Volkswagen. She was worried because she couldn't see the driver. Maybe that was because there was no driver. She hadn't paid attention while backing up, and her bumper snagged the VW, towing it several miles north of the city.

Needless to say, the man got his car back. The woman received a ticket for inattention. I hate being followed by yellow Volkswagens, don't you?

"Following orders" is a term that should never be taken lightly. And it is not always a good idea to take orders literally—word for word, I mean. While sitting at my desk one day, one of the detectives rushed over to me, pointed to the back interview room, and said "Watch the door in case the prisoner tries to get out."

He did not say, "Watch the prisoner." He said "Watch the door."

So, I watched the door. No one tried to get past me. What I didn't know was that the prisoner had climbed out of the back window, scaled down the side of the building and escaped. All the while his brother had escaped the very same way from the Sheriff's office a couple of miles away.

So like I mentioned, "literal" is not necessarily a good thing.

After a full fledged county-wide APB (all points bulletin), turned out they had kidnapped two of our officers, stolen their guns, and left them handcuffed out in the boonies. After a long manhunt and trained dogs hot on the trail, both officers were recovered and the perpetrators arrested. The officers were embarrassed, cold, and somewhat miffed at me, but ok. I did not get in trouble. They realized I was blonde.

Sometimes weirdness reigns over a city. One week an airplane landed on the freeway. The same week an officer accidentally shot a hole in the wall at the police department. You never knew what would happen next.

That same week the FBI alarm went off. We sent officers immediately. They found a man inside the office. They shouted with guns drawn, "Up against the wall!" The policemen shoved him into the wall with fresh paint. The man was an FBI agent who forgot to turn off the alarm. He wasn't having a good week, either. He had to return home and change his clothes. Dark suit and beige paint didn't go together.

There were times when humor was the only answer for a cranky customer, even if it was accidental. We were taught to maintain control of all situations. Well, great, sometimes that's out of our hands. Sometimes control can be maintained by making a fool out of yourself.

One afternoon a woman and her family angrily jerked open the auto-close door to my office. I noted her expression and knew she would probably tear my head off the minute she opened her mouth.

I pushed back my chair to get up. It caught on the rug and fell backward, leaving me in a heap on the floor, feet in the air, skirt up around my neck. I bounced up quickly, slapped the counter top, and out of my mouth came these words:

"So. How may I help you? I obviously can't help myself."

The entire entourage of angry people burst into near-hysterical laughter. As tears rolled down their faces, they simply turned around, walked out the door, and climbed the stairs to the parking ticket payment office. Apparently they got their revenge with my accident, as they paid the ticket without argument.

The caller sounded urgent. "A man with a gun looks angry and is stomping down the street towards a motel." I started to dispatch the call. The desk Sergeant stepped quickly into my radio room. I filled him in. He pointed at me and told me not to dispatch the call. I asked why. He told me to shut up and do what he said. As I filled out the radio log, a cold shiver ran up my spine.

Ten minutes passed. Another call came in. Someone had been murdered. A man with a gun had shot a Japanese man. It was one of the first "hate" crimes I encountered over my career. Nausea swept over me. We should have prevented it.

When confronted by the Captain, the desk Sergeant blamed it on me. He explained that I refused to dispatch. It was my word against his. They demanded a lie detector test for us both. I passed. He failed. They fired him, but all of that didn't matter anymore. Someone had lost his life and it was basically our fault. The depth of responsibility hit me like a freight train. This job was not a joke, it was important.

The boss wanted me to drive the meter wagon instead of walk the parking route. I was not proficient with a stick shift. The meter wagon (affectionately known as the "hoopy") was a three-wheeled monstrosity that easily tipped over or got caught in the railroad tracks in the middle of the street. The regular meter maid, Earline, tried valiantly to teach me. After several near catastrophes, she demanded that the boss stop whining about my driving and let me walk the route. She liked me fine, but she didn't want to see me wreck her beloved hoopy.

One of the final days of parking ticket patrol I was called to the scene of two motorcyclists parked illegally. From almost a block away, I noted that they were carrying guns. I was not armed. I approached and they backed up into an arrogant defense posture. Like a person with an unfriendly dog, I didn't make eye contact and just kept my vision focused with one eye on the guns and one eye on my ticket book.

"You'll have to move your vehicles. You are parked in a yellow zone too close to the intersection." Was I convincing? They stared angrily at me.

"I will report you to the patrol division if you do not comply." My voice was level, but my insides were jumping all over the place.

A slight sneer tried to creep across their faces. Did they know I was unarmed? Could they tell that I had no radio in my puffy uniform coat? Amazingly, they complied. I walked back to the office and tried to quit shaking. That situation was nerve-wracking, but the boss was proud of me for not flinching or freaking out. But at that moment, I decided that the office was probably a better choice for me.

"I don't understand. Why did he have to die?" Tears rolled down the man's face. One of his freshman college students hanged himself the night before. The family couldn't face walking into the police department to pick up his personal effects, so they asked the instructor to do it. My heart ached. I understood about suicidal thoughts.

As I tried to console the man at the counter, my own tears threatened to drip on the papers. My voice cracked. He needed comfort and I was leaking water all over the place. I was a big softy. For me, it was a wake-up call. I was a little too emotional for street work.

When regular female officers began to join the force, my officer certification was deactivated. Office work suited me better from an emotional strength point of view. The dream of being a street cop was fully dead. By the early 90's I had been promoted to a supervisory records position. The knowledge I gained from actual police and criminal justice courses gave me much needed help in that job.

You loved your job in spite of the problems of the daily routine. Things always work out for the good. Sometimes we can't see it at the time. Our dreams sometimes have to change.

> Yeah, Red. A tough street cop I was not. However, by the time
> I retired, some of the officers called me "Colonel" behind
> my back. Oh, well, at least I was tough at something.

CHAPTER 26

Marriage Lessons

IN THE EARLY years, my immediate supervisor introduced me to one of her friends and we hit it off. We ran off one weekend to my old church and the Pastor closed the deal in a hurry. My fiancé didn't want a fancy wedding. And we had decided all that family falderal was not worth it. So we had an after-wedding party instead.

Dad didn't like him at all. Mom was hopeful. She tried to stay positive. Dad was convinced that the man was a jerk, and that we would have problems. I thought they were over-reacting or mad because we didn't invite them to some big ceremony. I should have trusted their instincts.

I also should have taken the hint when one of the people at our party fell out of bed and broke his nose. I think it was a message.

My husband yelled easily. I yelled back. Once in a while we'd slap each other. I cried every day from his negative, harsh way of seeing life. Even with friends on the department, he told me he hated cops. His friends were fine; my friends evoked a shouting match. And yet, I loved him with all my heart.

The doctor once diagnosed me as pregnant. That evoked another fight. He didn't want children. I wanted at least one. It worked out, though, as the pregnancy failed before anything could "mess up" our lives.

To his family, Christmas was for exchanging cigarettes. But I didn't smoke, so too bad for me. Our friends had to force him into gifts, as generally he returned home drunk on Christmas Eve and had no plans to get any. I was pretty sure he loved me, but simply didn't have a clue how to do it. Knowing that did not make it easier.

We drank a lot. Too much, too often.

After seven years of marriage, I decided that maybe Daddy was right. Maybe there was a problem.

Many people make mistakes. They don't wait for the right person. They are blinded by loneliness or even because they think sex is love. And sometimes it's simply because they don't have a very good self-image, so they settle for someone who may be wounded in spirit. The river of life also brought you back around to a new husband later on, one that would be a restoration of all that was stolen by the first mistake.

CHAPTER 27

PTS and the Voice of Many Waters

THE PHONE RANG. Fear rushed through me. Frequently, my father-in-law would call just to shower me with horrible names. It nearly terrified me to answer the phone. I just let it ring.

I wondered how the marriage had gone so wrong. How did I miss the negative things?

I sank back into the easy chair. He wouldn't be home until after midnight, so I'd be safe for a few hours. My ankles hurt from the sprains. No more drinking. No more falling down a flight of stairs. This time I had learned that lesson.

The doorbell rang. I fought back the panic. Should I answer it? I took a deep breath and remembered that no one was home to know whether I went to the door or not. I hobbled to it.

It was Rosalie, our "vegetable" neighbor. She had a stack of books for me to read. I knew I was far "smarter" than her, because she was a little crazy. After all, I was a member of MENSA and had a high IQ. I wouldn't fall for that Christian stuff. Did I mention that sometimes people end up with their foot in their mouth with stupid judgments?

But she was friendly and charming, and her smile lit up my dark corner of the world, so I accepted the books. It was something to do.

Rosalie left for home and I perused the books. They didn't seem very interesting, just a lot of Christian mumbo-jumbo. It was time for my favorite TV show, so I flipped on the set and grabbed a soda from the frig.

I thumbed through one of the books while watching my show, and suddenly realized that I had forgotten about the TV. The words grabbed my heart. A man was loved in the book. He had a purpose. He knew God personally. Could I know God? Did I have a purpose? I wondered.

Golden Light broke through my thoughts and literally washed across the room. The lights were low in the house, but not in that room. Jinxie, our silver toy poodle scampered to the corner, and shook like he'd seen a ghost. He could sense something supernatural had just occurred! (He did see a ghost, by the way, it was the Holy Ghost).

The Voice rippled through the living room like a rushing stream. "I have room for you in My plan. I love you." I cried, and sang, and laughed. The Creator of the Universe loved me! I was free. The hours passed with joy. I was different. I had a new tomorrow. At that moment, I joined the vegetable garden.

By 1 a.m. my husband arrived home. He stomped in the door in an angry mood. His eyes twitched in circles, and didn't hold a straight line. There was no smell of alcohol, so I knew he wasn't drunk. The eyes frightened me.

He almost growled. "Now that you have the warmth of *God*, you don't need anything from me." How did he know what happened? I hadn't told him! The word "demons" came to mind.

Months passed. Tongue lashings became the norm at our house. "You're fat and ugly!" "You're having an affair; you're not really going to church, are you?"

I felt the need to scrub the floor each time before I left the house so that he wouldn't yell so much. Fear tried to overtake me, pushing me away from normal tasks like answering the door or the phone. Faith had to rise up and give me strength. I had God now. He loved me. However, I knew that PTS—Post Traumatic Stress—had set in and I needed to leave. So in the spring of 1980, the marriage dissolved.

Fear ruins people's lives. A bad marriage can kill you. God never wants such an unpleasant atmosphere for those He loves. His purpose for His children is peace. By leaving you gained a precious friend for life-Rosalie.

Yes, Red. And by the way, my ex-husband became a Christian later in life. I was very happy for him!

CHAPTER 28

More Broken Dreams

I HATED BEING ALONE again, although I had a good church and many Christian friends. I thought maybe one day we would all "go into ministry" together. Maybe they would be my future. One morning, Mom and I decided to visit Pastor and his family.

When we pulled into the parking lot a strangely eerie feeling gripped us both. The church was empty. No cars in the lot, and no lights in the church. The parish houses looked empty too. What happened?

We checked the Pastor's house. Their car was in the driveway and the door was open, but no one responded to our knock. So we walked in.

Pastor, his wife and all the kids were huddled in the bedroom. Their eyes were red from crying.

There was a sorrow in the pastor's face that I will never forget. He advised us that the entire church, with the exception of two people, had been cajoled into moving away with another pastor to Texas. It's called sheep-stealing, and in this case, it destroyed the church and a family. Now there would be no money coming in to pay the mortgages or car payments. They were literally alone with no means of support. Pastor would have to find a secular job.

My heart ached. There was no future here for anyone. I drove home in tears. Their hearts were broken, and so was mine. They were still my friends and I would stand with them. But I had a terrific sense of lost hope for the future. I knew we would survive, but I wondered about my own future with God. It seemed to fade into the distance.

Ministry is where you find it, not in a church building or a group of people. It isn't about a big name, or even a title. It's about loving people where they are at the moment. And if you have your hopes pinned to people, you will be disappointed. People will always fail you. Need to keep your hope in God. Sounds like that was a hard lesson to learn.

Yes, Red. A hard lesson.

CHAPTER 29
Fiji the First Time

I NEEDED A VACATION, a rest from the stress in my life. Some friends told me about a place in the South Pacific with lovely people and interesting history. My savings account would have to be emptied to go there, but it was worth it to get away. So Fiji was the destination, and my college advisor agreed to give me extra class credits for any papers I might do in the process.

The Townhouse apartments in downtown Suva were to be my home for three weeks. We deplaned in Nadi, the international airport of the islands. Tropical birds flew around inside the airport terminal! And there were people with goats and sheep sitting in the waiting area.

The hot, humid air hit me like a furnace, and the smell of the rain forest smelled like a sack of garbage that had not been taken out for a while. But the sights and sounds made up for it. There were different races — Asian and East Indian descent as well as Native Fijians. The country had recently undergone a military coup. As I noted the different races, I wondered what had precipitated the situation. I hoped it wasn't racial, but the thought plagued me.

The man at customs stared at my blond hair. His questions were personal, not luggage related. He was not in a hurry, so I missed the connecting flight to Suva. I approached the ticket agent and asked when the next flight out would be. Eleven hours to wait. The prospect of sleeping in the open-air terminal with the goats and sheep didn't appeal to me.

A few minutes later, he called me to the ticket desk. I could ride in a taxi with some others who also missed their flight. Ok. A 200 mile taxi ride in the heat. Oh, great.

Three of us and our entire luggage jammed into the taxi. No air conditioning in about 98% humidity. Goody. The man in the back seat with me was Sam from Saipan. We chit-chatted about Saipan. I had heard of Saipan in geography class, but had no recollection of where it was.

The man in front was English, a Mr. Bill Wilson. His business brought him to Fiji often, so he knew his way around. The fear of being alone started to creep in.

Green iguanas skittered across the windy road. Fiji had no natural predators on land, just brightly hued tropical birds and iguanas. I had always loved wildlife, even if it wasn't very cuddly.

As we talked, I suddenly worried about being alone. I asked Mr. Wilson for his number in Fiji, just in case something bad happened. He was hesitant, but felt sorry for this chicken-livered traveler, so handed me his business card.

We finally arrived in Suva. The hotel apartments were modest, but perfectly livable. No TV, though, just a radio that picked up the BBC in Australia. I saw very few white people and no white ladies alone. I began to wonder if I had made a serious mistake.

I decided to take a walk up the street near the hotel. A leathery-skinned elderly woman was bent over, using a machete bigger than she was to hack out the unwanted foliage from her front yard. When standing straight, she came up to my chest. She was a tiny thing who could wield a machete with swift, deadly accuracy. I did not want to make her mad, but I had to have a photo. I asked her if I could take a picture. She smiled with a toothless grin, chopped off a frangipane flower and stuck it behind her ear for the pose. She was adorable.

However, as I finished with Madame Machete, I noticed that an entourage of men had gathered behind me. It was extremely uncomfortable to have several men following behind me like puppies. The hotel was about a block from the police station. Could I make a run for it?

I pushed open the front doors of the Townhouse. The men did not come inside. What a relief.

I wandered up to the restaurant at the hotel. The menu was interesting, but no American food. The menu was simply confusing.

"I can help you, Miss." A hefty Fijian man with a blue chef's jacket towered over my table. His wrists were twice the size of mine. "My name is Shamu and I am the chef here. Where are you from?"

"America. What is good to eat on your menu?" I had to speak slowly and carefully so they could understand me. I had an American accent. Must have done ok, as some of them thought I was from Australia.

"I will make you American food for lunch—you will love it. I will make you a grilled cheese sandwich with tomatoes. I make, you will like." He turned and ambled back to the kitchen.

The sandwich was perfect. He even put mayo on it. The cheese was gooey. My favorite. It wasn't so bad. I could eat there and be safe. That night I tried the "coconut chicken" with a Coca-Cola, of course. (For the duration of my stay, Shamu worked hard to take good care of his American customer. The only faux pas we had occurred the morning I sat on a giant cockroach. With the loud buzz of its wings and my screams, poor Shamu had to calm down the breakfast patrons. At least they weren't sleepy any more.)

By two days into the trip, it was clear that Mr. Wilson would not be needed, so I dropped his phone number in the garbage can. I decided to check out the police station, but first had to call and make an appointment with the Commissioner. The first stop was the open market on the way. I bought some "grog" (Kava) to give to the Police Commissioner as I had read it was a tradition. Best not to violate their customs.

I waited for the Commissioner. And waited. And waited. The appointment was for 10 A.M. But that meant about 12 P.M. South Pacific Time. When he finally arrived, we drank grog in the traditional way, from a half of a coconut shell. He granted me permission to interview any of his men at any shift. I had full access to the department, so decided to start the interviews that night.

Sgt. Esaias (Isaiah) was introduced and assigned to me. He promised that no one would hurt me while I was in Suva. He told me to run to the department any time with any problem and the police would take care of me. He even invited me to a weekend concert to see their Swing Band and meet the head of their country! What an honor.

That night, I sauntered down to the police department to meet up with their night shift detectives. The night shift Lieutenant advised me that he was there if I ever needed any help. They treated me like a queen. The resident Interpol Officer interviewed me first. Apparently, he had to make sure I wasn't dangerous. I must have been quite dull, as within five minutes he was bored and wandered out the door without saying goodbye.

The night shift detectives and I drank grog together. Stuff tasted like dirty dishwater, but it seemed to give me freedom to talk to the men.

They told me that there was rampant racism. They said that Indians were hated. Some of the Indians told me that Natives were vicious and had beaten them just because of their race. The Natives said that the Indians were thieves. I was shocked. That's why the military coup. They hated each other. All of this was based on the differing cultures and racial types. I said goodnight and retired to the hotel. Hatred because of race had never been logical to me. I had much to think about.

In the middle of the night, an uproar outside awakened me. The sound of breaking glass and shouting ramped up for about a half an hour; then everything fell silent. I stayed in my room and minded my own business.

Morning dawned. A riot had broken out one street away when an Indian business was burned. No one was killed, but a couple lost their livelihood. For what?

Saturday Concert time rolled around. I met Esaias at the department. We walked (very slowly) to the park. It seemed no one in Fiji was ever in a hurry to be on time.

The concert was set up with folding chairs and a portable stage. The Sergeant introduced me to Sitiveni Rabuka, the General in charge of Fiji. He reminded me of a huge cedar tree! His wrists were even bigger than Shamu's. He shook my hand. I expected crushed fingers. But no. He knew his strength. The handshake was perfect—strong, but not overpowering. The man was not a fool.

The Swing Band and their lively music brought everyone in the park to their feet. They laughed and clapped at the boisterous music. Even the staunch military head of state swayed to the beat of the band. When the concert concluded, Sgt. Esaias walked back with me to the police department.

Sunday arrived and it was time to go to church. Since I was attending an Assembly of God fellowship at home off and on, I wanted to go there. But the Methodists had blockaded the roads to force a Sabbath. Nobody drove on Sunday, and definitely no taxies or buses. So I walked across the street to the Catholic Cathedral.

The people were exceptionally friendly. I was hugged by everyone and kissed by the Priests. That shook me up a bit, but learned quickly that in some countries, "holy kisses" were still given freely. One of the nuns, Sister Irene, invited me to the Sisters of Cluny convent for breakfast and prayers. One of the Priests invited me to a Rotary Club meeting next week in the afternoon. Rotary Club? In Fiji? I was pretty sure that was a men only group.

Some of the congregation were Charismatic and invited me to a meeting in the basement of the Cathedral later in the week. I was no longer alone!

The first appointment arrived. Sister Irene drove me down Waimanu Road to the convent. Waimanu Road had some extreme curves in it, the kind a normal driver should take at about 25 mph. Not Sister Irene. She drove like a race car driver at Monte Carlo.

We stopped at the white buildings of the Convent. The atmosphere was warm and comfortable. Flame trees with brilliant orange blossoms towered over the road. Frangipane trees with fragrant white blooms greeted us at the Convent door. It was an atmosphere of prayer and love.

They served fresh papaya and pineapple juice for breakfast. A person could get used to that. The Nuns were filled with joy and peace, and their breakfast mood was filled with laughter and teasing. Many of the ladies had been there for many years, ministering to everyone. Sister Irene invited me to stay in Fiji with them. She mentioned that I had a call on my life. While it was tempting, the idea of living on a small island so far from home did not appeal to me. She was right about the call, however, something I would not learn until years later.

She led me into the prayer chapel where sunlight poured through the windows. Fresh cut flowers on the altar released perfume into the air. God was definitely there—and it was a place where He was honored and loved. I spent a little time in prayer to soak up the atmosphere. When time was up, Sister Irene returned me to the hotel. She drove a little slower going back. She had probably noticed my white knuckles and fingernails digging themselves into the dash of her car.

The Charismatic Catholic meeting was in the basement of the Cathedral across from the hotel. Their exuberance for worship and their love of God encouraged me. We even knew some of the same choruses. New friends had been made, and the people of Fiji had become a part of my heart.

Their speaker for the evening was Father Kenneth Metz from the Vatican. I'd never have met him in America, as the distances were simply too great. We chatted for a while after the service and learned that we had a mutual friend. It served to remind me that the world was much smaller than most of us think.

A few days later and it was time for the Rotary Club meeting at my hotel's bar. The men greeted me with joy. No woman ever had been allowed to attend one of the meetings. They all tried to buy me a beer at once, which became an interesting situation. I said no, just Coke. The bartender laughed. She had been buying Coke at an alarming rate due to my constant orders.

Their speaker for the day was the French Ambassador to the South Pacific. He spoke about nuclear testing. He claimed America was evil and wanted to conquer France. His stance was that France had to test in the ocean because America was planning attack them. I kept thinking the guy had lost his mind. And I wasn't alone.

One of the priests from the church called him on it. He advised the Ambassador that his ideas were far-fetched. He was adamant that France was hurting the coral reefs and wildlife. Of course, the Ambassador denied it. He justified himself by stating Jacques Cousteau agreed with the tests.

Nobody believed him. I wrote down what he said and took it back to the states. I would find out the truth when I got home.

As I packed up after the three week adventure, I felt a deep sadness at leaving my new friends. Their openness to my presence and questions, their faith and their joy were contagious. While the racism issue pervaded their society, as individuals they had endeared themselves to my heart. As I said goodbye to the bartender, she shook my hand and said, "I think that we will miss you around here." I hope she wasn't stuck with twenty cases of Coke after I left.

Upon arrival at home, my first order of business was to write a letter to Jacques Cousteau and learn the truth about nuclear testing in the

South Pacific. He sent me volumes of research against it, and was fit to be tied that the French Ambassador would say the he was in favor of it. I suspect a head rolled on that issue.

People should always seek truth. Just because an "important person" says so, doesn't make it true!

Boy, Red, you are right on that one.

CHAPTER 30
Hope Deferred

AFTER BEING HOME for a few weeks, I began to note a serious change in a boyfriend I had been dating for about 4 years. He was smart and handsome, and we loved cooking and going to church. He drifted away slowly, and eventually stopped calling or dropping by. I knew in the back of my mind that it was because he didn't believe in marriage, as he believed positively that all marriages ended in divorce, but it was still a sort of rejection that caused deep heartache.

My home was the place where the remnants of our church held services. That, too, slowly drifted into oblivion as Pastor and his wife became estranged. My heart was sick, as Scripture would say. The final straw came when he had a severe heart attack. Ministry was too stressful. So after recovery, he and his wife finalized their divorce. His wife, my friend, also abandoned the area. Eventually he moved away, and went back to college to get a post-graduate degree. I was angry. I had invested a significant amount of emotion and service in the church, and it was completely gone.

Bitterness began to set in. It reached a fever pitch when word came that he had remarried to someone who had once been my friend. I felt betrayed. As far as I was concerned, Christians were the ultimate hypocrites. I hated them. I still thought I loved God, but had no clue that my bitterness would eventually destroy my faith if I let it continue. I also did not understand that hatred is the opposite of love for God.

Along came an old friend, Siony and her adopted Mom, Lue. As members of one of the large Assembly of God churches in the area, they saw that I was in trouble and dragged me kicking and screaming to their fellowship. I had attended that fellowship on occasion, but not regularly. Now I was forced into the pew to sit and think about my plight. Perhaps I would be able to hide there and not do anything. That lasted about a week.

Remember what I said about pinning your hopes on people? When you have a personal agenda that is dependent upon people, it will always fail. And I'm glad you went to that church, because it was there that you not only got all healed up, you were able to become a worship leader, a drama coach and actress, and your voice got stronger. You learned how to worship from deep in your spirit. I'm sure you finally forgave everyone, right?

I forgave them all Red. You'll see later.

SECTION 5

Fresh Horizons

CHAPTER 31

Joshua and Mom

MOM'S BELOVED DOG Spunky died horribly when the mail carrier hit a slick spot and lost control of her mail truck. Mom was broken-hearted and inconsolable. She was also alone during the day while I was at work, which worried me. I wanted to get her a new dog, but she was so grieved she would yell at me when I mentioned it.

One weekend, I wandered into the Safeway store in Sandpoint, Idaho. There was a cardboard box by the door. Never, never look into any cardboard box by the entrance to a grocery store. It will be your undoing. You will go home with a furry, four-footed waif.

The box contained 6 Newfoundland puppies. Newfys are not really bears, but for the amount of times people asked me if I owned a bear cub, I think they almost qualify. I reached into the box and one of them literally wrapped his paws around my arm and would not let go. That was all it took—he came home with me.

The dog loved riding in the car. He climbed all over me on the way home. I named him "Joshua" after one of my favorite heroes of the Bible.

Mom's initial reaction was unfavorable... no, angry. She didn't want another dog. She missed Spunky. That was another thing that lasted about a week. I came home from work one day and Josh was lying on Mom's couch all wrapped up in her robe, his legs dangling over the edge. She thought he was cold. His loving character won her over. Or it could have been the sight of a bear-like puppy staggering around the house with a lampshade on his head. He ate the first five books of my expensive leather Bible too. He was quite spiritual, don't you think?

Joshua had a penchant for stealing the neighbor's food off the grill. The neighbors weren't particularly happy about us owning a master thief. The hysterical sight of a big fuzzy black puppy bolting down the country road with a large loaf of French bread firmly gripped in his teeth was entertaining. How can you be mad at that? And besides, bread wasn't the only victim. Throw rugs, boots, socks, anything left unattended on porches was fair game. Speaking of kleptomaniac... And where did it all go? The pile in the back yard, that's where. My neighbors threatened me often.

In an attempt to restrain our master thief, we tied him up with a logging chain. For the uninitiated, a logging chain has links that would take a caterpillar tractor to break. Well, a tractor or a Newfoundland. He managed to break the chain enough times that I finally gave up and left him in the house while I was at work.

As time passed, Joshua grew to 135 pounds of pure muscle. He took very good care of us. No strangers came to our house more than once. He would lunge against the screen door if he didn't like you and scare the living daylights out of people.

Mom progressively grew weaker. One night she hurt so bad that she overdosed on Tylenol. The ambulance was called and they pumped her stomach. But the social worker at the hospital said she had to go to assisted living. I could not care for her 24 hours a day, so she needed to be somewhere under supervision. She did not want to go.

I found a nice care facility in a home with 24 hour care. Even though I was able to see her every day, and even bring Josh to visit, her health went downhill fast.

With Mom gone from the premises, the landlord gave me notice that I had to move out. Mom was his friend, but he could no longer allow me to stay at the low rent I had been paying. On my meager salary the $600 a month upgrade was too high. So I hunted for a rental that would allow big dogs.

As the deadline approached, I started to worry. Landlords did not want a pet bear in their buildings. Just a few short days before the end of the month, a friend called. They knew someone who would take us! And the price was low. The tiny old house had no amenities and had a cracked foundation, but it was a place to live. I took it. Turned out the landlord fell in love with Joshua the moment she laid eyes on him and bought herself a Newfy named Duke. So of course we could live in their rental!

One night after the move, I went to visit Mom. She didn't feel well that day. Her veins were distended and she seemed extremely weak. My former boyfriend dropped by that evening and chatted with her for a while. He called to tell me they had a great conversation about me being all right even if we weren't together any more. The resident doctor told him that she had pneumonia.

Morning dawned and the phone rang. It was the doctor. Mom had died in the night. It wasn't pneumonia, it was congestive heart failure. She had finally let go of life, believing that I would get through whatever the future held.

I would miss her, and still miss her today. In spite of the usual kid versus Mom issues, she was my shadow and friend. It was strangely comforting to take her out for an ice cream, or take her to church with me. She had spent her life lifting me up, supporting my school activities, in general making certain that I would succeed at anything. Her character had been impeccable, her sense of humor dry, and her fondness for practical jokes had seeped into my life on occasion. Even Joshua mourned her passing by squeezing himself next to me as tight as possible while I grieved.

She was the best Mom in the world. I wish everyone could have a Mom like mine.

One of the first Ten Commandments says, "Honor your father and your mother; that it may go well with you in the earth." Most humans seem to carry grudges and blame their parents. But they have a choice. You had a choice. Life or death, humans can choose.

You're the best, Red.

CHAPTER 32
A Keeper

AFTER A SHORT sabbatical, I returned to college to work on completion of my second degree in Criminal Justice. Working full time and carrying a full load of night classes was a good way to focus after Mom's death. It was also exhausting, but when you've just lost friends and family, it's better than the pity party method.

One evening at the beginning of the semester, all of the students for Ethics class stood in the hallway waiting for the door to open. One of them was a gentle-spirited man named Myron. His eyes grabbed me — they were almost identical to the eyes of my dog! No kidding, this man had dark brown puppy eyes. As we chatted, I learned that his mother had recently died too. I also learned that we had many of the same classes.

It seemed like I had known Myron forever. He fit, sort of like an old pair of house slippers... comfortable. But after having been hurt before, I was wary and unsure. He would stand by the bus stop at the college and wait for me to arrive for classes... even if it was raining or snowing. He didn't have a car, only a motorcycle. One day he rode that motorcycle 45 miles in a blinding snowstorm to buy me a silk scarf for Christmas. I was slowly beginning to think he might be "the one."

Of course, I had to check it out with the dog. Joshua was a great protector, peeing on one date, scratching another, and snarling at the rest. So I accepted a first date with Myron and opened the door to see what would happen.

Joshua sniffed Myron fully and took in all his "energy." He wagged his tail. Myron sat down on the couch. Joshua licked his hand. Myron stroked his fur. That was it. They were fast friends in all of two minutes. Now the only hurdle left was God. If He said yes, it was a done deal.

A few weeks later Myron went with me to a Christian women's meeting. Our guest for the evening was a local Country-Western singer. He sang old fashioned gospel songs, and Myron began to weep. My friend Lue prayed with Myron to receive the Lord in a more deeply personal way than he thought possible. God apparently said yes. He was definitely "the one."

Joshua knew ahead of time. Didn't I tell you that "dog" is "God" spelled backwards?

CHAPTER 33

Wedding Madness

MYRON SNAGGED ME one day after work and drove me to a local park. It was a warm summer evening. The sun radiated through the trees by the lake, leaving rays of light sprinkled around the grass. He dropped to his knees and asked, "Will you marry me?"

Oh, yes. We kissed in full view of the world. The love in his eyes penetrated my heart. He was honest and kind. His kids, Dana and Jerry were wonderful. His ex-wife was a very nice lady. We all got along well. We started to plan our wedding at the church. THIS man was not afraid of being married in front of all our family and friends.

We drove to Copper Mountain, a favorite Huckleberry area in North Idaho. I'm sure the bears didn't care that we borrowed their favorite smorgasbord. We scrambled up a craggy piece of granite and perched there to survey the view of the Idaho Mountains. Winding rivers and pristine lakes dotted the landscape, leaving us with the impression of an infinite wilderness. Our lives promised a perpetual display of the view from the summit. That's where we wanted to stay… at the summit.

December rolled around and we decorated the church with cream, yellow, and peach flowers. It was a touch of spring in winter. Good thing the inside was bright and cheery, because it was raining, no, pouring outside. All of our families and friends had dressed up only to be greeted with splashes of sloppy water and an occasional dollop of mud.

My brother Richard was there to walk me down the aisle. Dad panicked at the thought of walking into a church, so pawned off the job on my brother. I had promised him that the roof wouldn't cave in on him, but he wouldn't trust it.

Myron's grand-niece Hailey sat down on the steps to the balcony and immediately pulled her skirt over her head. No religious junk in that kid. It broke the ice. Everyone relaxed and laughed at her antics.

The ceremony started and it was instantly obvious that the sound system wasn't working. Pastor looked up at the sound booth to find it empty. No one had assigned a technician for the ceremony! A quick run to the office and a frantic phone call and our friend Vanessa burst through the door and ran up to the sound booth.

As we started the first musical solo, we also noted that the microphones were set wrong for a guitar. She hadn't the time to fix it. My friend Del and I sang anyway. I had no idea what key he was singing in, and I couldn't hear him, but we muddled through. Winging it eventually became the most common method of operation for nearly everything in my life.

Myron and I stood together, holding hands during the vows. Jerry, Myron's son, was the Best Man, and Edythe, my Native American friend was the Matron of Honor. Nobody was throwing up, so we thought we were home free. That is, until Pastor told us to look at each other instead of stare at him.

He whispered, "You need to look at each other, not me."

Uh,oh. We knew that was going to be a problem. We choked our way through the wedding vows, and couldn't see Pastor for the tears.

Then Pastor teared up too. We all blubbered and coughed our way to the finish. What is it about weddings? Everybody turns into mung.

When it came time to throw the bouquet, there was only one choice in my mind. So instead of pitching it into the fray, I handed it to my friend Siony. She was next to find a husband, I was very certain. So why bother to throw it and maybe wreck the flowers? [Note: she did get married a couple of years later.]

The reception was held at our little rental house. It was still pouring rain and our house was far smaller than the church. I don't know what possessed us to have it at home instead of rent a building somewhere. I also had a brain gap and wrote out all the invitations different—some said bring gifts, some said don't bring gifts. I also for some stupid reason thought I could handle all the hostess duties and cut the cake too. Silly me.

By the time we managed to get most of the guests jammed into the house, I realized that there were too many tasks ahead of me to finish and still actually talk to the guests. Two of the girls from my office, Becky and Chris, volunteered to cut and serve the cake. Thank goodness. They literally saved me from disaster.

After everyone left, Myron and I prepared to leave for the honeymoon. We had spent the last of my savings account for the trip. Even though Myron did not yet have a job, somehow we knew it would work out.

Part of restoration is celebration. You started the marriage off with memories and celebration, a far cry from the first time. And I assume you locked Joshua in the bedroom or something during the festivities? Poor dog. He missed the cake leftovers.

It's ok, Red. Joshua got even by eating an entire box of Tums out of my suitcase before we left. The vet said that he probably wouldn't have indigestion for a long time.

SECTION 6
Survival Training

CHAPTER 34

Mexico

THE PLANE BANKED over Mexico City and landed on the runway. I don't remember ever seeing a city that big, but maybe it was the view from the plane that did it. We hailed a taxi, but after squishing ourselves inside the ancient looking back seat, began to regret our choice.

"Yo hablo Inglais?" We inquired. We thought he nodded, but weren't sure. Our funds were limited, so we hoped we were correct in the assumption. We showed him the itinerary that listed the hotel name and off we flew. I say flew because, whoa, Nellie, those taxi drivers were a little heavy on the throttle.

The taxi lurched away from the curb. In mid-flight, we realized that the exhaust fumes were sucking up all the air in the back seat! The window stuck as we tried to roll it down. As we coughed and tried to hold our breath, the driver assured us everything was fine. Yep, we might have forgotten to train for deep sea diving with no air tanks for the vacation, so I'm sure it was fine.

The car screeched to a stop in front of a big pink hotel. Mexicans seemed to like a lot of pink. Pink restaurants, pink hotels, pink theaters, pink everywhere. Huh. We scrambled out of the taxi, picked out our bags and handed him a tip. The tip wasn't much, but appeared to be more than the driver expected. He was all smiles as the taxi pulled away from the curb.

"Hasta la vista!" He shouted as he waved goodbye. It wasn't until much later that we learned about the exchange rate. We gave him a lot of money in his country. He probably had a steak dinner that night with all his friends.

We checked in and left our bags in the room. Since there was a zoo nearby, we decided to take a little side trip. We walked by the cages. Something rubbed me the wrong way. It wasn't a "zoo," it was a prison. The animals were crowded into enclosures that had no space whatsoever, and my temper was beginning to flare. The crocodiles and caimans had only a tiny bit of water and space in their enclosure. Anger rose to my face. Myron pulled me toward the entrance before I lost it and started an international incident. Cruelty to animals had always been a pet peeve of mine. Myron probably saved me from a stint in a Mexican jail.

Back at the hotel, coffee in the café was supremely romantic. The Spanish tile floor surrounded an open arboretum of orange flowers and dark green vines that hung from brightly colored hand painted clay pots all around the dining area. We could hear screeches and chirps of the tropical birds outside. I calmed down and moved back into "honeymoon" mode with a better outlook on the day to come.

Next morning the ride to the airport was easy, and we didn't have any near-death experiences from asphyxiation. Yippee.

The plane trip was short, but scenic. An almost flat topography wrapped in jungle seemed to stretch forever. The countryside didn't appear to have many people, and only a few plumes of smoke swirled up from the clumps of civilization below.

The plane circled over the tropical landscape and landed on an airstrip. It was basically dirt and a few globs of grass. We wondered where the actual airport was, as all we could see was a lone windsock hanging dejectedly from a pole in the middle of the "runway."

"Over there," the flight attendant pointed to a low, flat-roofed building near the edge of the forest. It was nothing like any terminal we had ever seen. There were lots of tourists inside, but amenities were decidedly missing.

We grabbed a taxi to the hotel. The ride was a tad bumpy, but no problem. As we drove into Merida, we realized that air quality was iffy—the streets were packed with diesel burning buses that had no mufflers. We glanced at each other and wondered if the room at the hotel was going to stink from exhaust.

We needn't have worried. The hotel was old style Spanish architecture with an open courtyard, and carved water fountain in the center. It was as if we had stepped back in time to a "hacienda" from some grand romantic movie.

After unpacking, we noted the hotel had a charming little pool. So we decided a nice swim and a beer afterwards would be fun. What we did not know was that most Mexican pools were not heated like American ones. We changed clothes and ran out back to dive in.

We had no intention of joining the "Polar Bear Club." My body instantly stiffened up and I had to force myself to breathe. Myron, being the intrepid diver anyway, just swam to the ladder and got out as if nothing was wrong. The men at the bar thought it was hysterical to watch the American woman scream upon her ungainly entrance into the icy water. They were still laughing even after we finished our drink and retired to the room. At least I could give someone a laugh for the day.

In Merida at Christmas time, la familias, or families were honored with wonderful events in the parks. Little children and parents strolled together through holiday decorations and vendors in brightly colored costumes. Red and white balloons hung on the vendor's stalls; shiny gold and silver Christmas tinsel was wrapped expertly around the hedges of flowers in the park. Taco stands and flower stalls were woven through the fun-filled landscape. Mariachi bands sang their lively music in the background. It was a Mexican festival of Christmas joy!

A flower lady spoke to Myron as we sauntered through the park. "Su esposa muy hermosa." Myron's Spanish was rusty, so he couldn't remember what that meant. I did. It meant "your wife is pretty." She had never seen me before makeup in the morning. Lucky her.

I thanked her with a quick, "Gracias," and explained that we were on our honeymoon. She smiled and put a small flower behind my ear. What a nice lady.

Days passed and we finally became experts at the monetary exchange rate. So much so, that Myron learned how to talk a poor Mexican child down from his two peso per sale income. There were lots of salesmen of all ages hawking everything from "hammacas" to thingamajigs that we couldn't fathom. Everyone seemed to be trying to make an American buck.

We stopped by the coffee shop on the corner in the middle of downtown. A man approached. We figured it was another salesman, so we prepared to say no. But it was something different this time. He knelt by the table.

"Are you Christians?" he asked politely.

We exchanged glances. We nodded. "Yes."

He extended his hand. "My name is Jose. I want to invite you to our fellowship today. Please come. And would you pray for me?"

He took us behind a nearby billboard. My suspicious nature made me watch carefully. But he was genuine. He explained that sometimes Pentecostals were persecuted by some of the local Catholics, so he just wanted to be safe for the prayer.

We prayed, he wept. He remarked that he really felt the Presence of the Lord, so he led us over to his car and drove to his fellowship. It was actually a birthday party! The men were gathered in the living room, the women in the kitchen. They were not allowed to fellowship together and the women had to eat last. But the pastor asked me to stay with the men. Not much English was spoken there. But we understood a couple of words off and on.

Everyone sang happy birthday in Spanish. Pastor gave a short sermon before the cake and presents. The men honored us as special and asked me for a word. I picked out a Scripture from their Bible. We enjoyed cake together while the women peered out from the kitchen as I was served with the men. They had never seen such a thing. It was quite an honor!

The man who brought us sang a special gospel song. He had a powerful, lovely voice. We all prayed. It was obvious that they needed Bibles. We offered money, but they refused. We were guests. They would not take, only give. But they valued our prayers. Why can't more of us be like that?

Our new friend drove us back to the hotel. By then it was dark. He walked us inside the hotel. Just as we opened the door, we saw some balloons drifting along the sidewalk. He grabbed them for his "ninos." Our hearts broke. It was Christmas. He had no presents for his children, his "ninos."

We asked if there was something we could do to help him. He refused any money. We were his new friends. He did not take from friends. He worked, though, so perhaps we would buy something from his workplace. We purchased a shirt. I insisted on giving him a shawl for his wife. He thanked us for our loving kindness. We prayed a final prayer and he left us. We occasionally spotted him at the coffee shop after that, which turned out to be owned by his brother. I resolved to send him some Bibles when I returned home.

As our journey moved swiftly toward time to return to the US, we decided to take a trip to the Mayan ruins at Chichen-Itza. It was the only tourist thing in our plan, and we were pretty excited. Being a rockhound is often closely related to archeology and paleontology, so we were ready for the ancient past to come alive.

On the way we stopped at an Agave factory. The temperature had started to climb, so by the time we arrived at the factory, the stench of the smashed plants could have knocked you over. So this was the beginnings of tequila. The image of grub worms crawling around fermenting plant juice cured me of any desire for that particular alcohol. But it was interesting.

Back on the bus, the road curved deep into the jungle. We could see the pyramid sticking out of the canopy. The bus driver told a story about a jade cat deep inside the corridors of the structure. I would have liked to see that… until the tour guide mentioned that there were no lights and it was dark and dangerous in the tunnels. Not a good choice for claustrophobic or "spider-shy" people.

The ancient city overwhelmed our senses with Mayan history. We decided to climb the pyramid. I mean to say, Myron wanted to climb the pyramid. I stared up at the steep stairs. The steps were the width of my foot (sideways), about 18 or more inches apart and moved skyward at about an 80 degree angle. No handholds, either. Those Mayans had to be really tall to climb the steps. I made it up 3 of them before vertigo set in. I slid backwards on my hind end and waited for Myron to return. He made it all the way to the top. Tough cookie, that husband of mine.

You are the consummate animal lover that you could care about crocodilians in a cage. And the experiences with Jose have the imprint of Divine encounter on them. The poverty rampant throughout the earth is difficult to watch for many. God charges people with taking care of the widows and orphans of the world, but people prefer to do it without actual contact, if they do it at all. Sad, that. And I hope that in the future you will be able to take more risks without fear. I assume you remembered the Bibles?

Yes, Red. I remembered the Bibles. But I think I'll leave climbing pyramids to Myron.

CHAPTER 35

Waterlogged

MYRON DECIDED TO take a day trip to show me where he had grown up. We loaded up Joshua the Newfy into the back of the pickup, and set out on the adventure. Cataldo, Myron's childhood home, is a very small town on the Coeur d'Alene River in Northern Idaho. It is also near the banks of a wide creek called LaTour Creek. Now, that particular Creek floods every spring from snow melt. Did I mention it was spring? So we ventured up the hillside by the creek to see his old homestead.

Myron is intrepid, nothing slows him down. Much. Except perhaps a torrent of flood waters. Latour Creek had overflowed its banks and was running a few feet above the channel. He revved the engine to cross the usually shallow water, but hit a bump and the engine stalled. Within seconds, water rushed through the cab and the pickup would not restart.

While Myron hiked across the road to his cousin's house for help, Joshua the dog forced his hairy black body through the window to the cab and kathunked onto the seat to rescue Mommy. A few big slurps across my face and he was fine. Me, on the other hand, I was not so good.

Negative possibilities flooded my mind like the water rushing through the pickup. It was deep in there, too. My mind, I mean. And I was afraid to open the door of the truck for fear the water would completely inundate us. So, of course, I started whining to God.

Now here is a tip: prayers of desperation are heard by God, but He prefers you to have some sort of trust in His abilities. The "Help, God, we're drowning" routine may prolong the worrisome circumstances.

A strange sense of peace was with me, but my teeth were clenched from anxiety, and my knuckles white from grasping the dog's collar. When Myron returned, the only thought I could muster was, "Yay, Lord, we're rescued, we can go home now."

God snickered. I should have known.

Myron's cousin pulled us out of the hole. Then Myron revved the engine and navigated across the stream as if there were no flood. We drove FORWARD, instead of backwards. Hey! Wait a minute! That meant we would have to cross it yet one more time later! It also was a harbinger of things to come in our lives, and an important lesson: take ground and don't give it up to go backwards. You don't learn to overcome by going backwards. Sigh.

We drove to the old homestead location, a lovely meadow with a magnificent view of Idaho's majestic mountains. After an hour or so of romping in the tall grass and wildflowers, we climbed back in the pickup and forged our way back through the creek and on to the road. No harm, no foul. The water really did not overflow us, although at first blush it looked like we were goners. And … there was a strange sense of victory over bad circumstances.

What I did not know at the time was that Myron had paid more attention to the configuration of the creek bottom after the engine stalled. He scoped it out and drove on the path that would be safe. I decided that my husband was going to take some getting used to.

A real lesson in trust, huh?

Yeah, Red and I'm not sure I've learned it yet.

CHAPTER 36
No Cars

THE ENTRANCE ROAD to Lake Foredyce in Northern California had an ominous sign on it. "This road not for cars," with a drawing of a car and a big red slash through it. We were driving a Subaru Justy—that was a tiny 4 wheel drive vehicle with a very small wheel base. Definitely classified as a "car."

We ignored the sign and drove past one jeep off-road vehicle with a broken driveline. The owner and his friends stared at us with that "they're gonna be in trouble" sneer on their faces as we clunked and thudded on up the road. And I use the word "road" loosely.

The "road" eventually gave way to ruts about four feet deep, and jagged rocks that jutted out from the center of the furrows. Myron maneuvered our little car to put the tires on just the bare edges of the rough stones. Had we slipped into the ruts, the car would have been smashed beyond repair, and we'd have been stuck sideways in a very precarious situation.

Slowly, expertly, he inched past the danger zone and we moved on into the camping area beside the Lake. I may have lost some enamel on my teeth from gritting them in the ordeal, but I have to say, that little

Justy was great. Turned out the wheel base was exactly the right width for the rocks. A larger vehicle might not have made it so easily. Myron knew that, by the way, he just loves to make me cringe.

The next morning, Myron woke us all up and announced that he had planned a hike around the lake. He promised it was a nice easy hike of about 3 or 4 miles just around the shoreline. Famous last words.

I packed my backpack with lots of water and snacks, grabbed a hat to protect my fair skin from the sun, and rubbed on the sun block lotion. Myron, his best friend Jerome, our daughter Dana, and I hiked off around the shore. If I had known what was ahead, I'd have stayed at camp with my feet up on a lawn chair. Of course, then I would have missed that trust lesson.

The hike wasn't bad, with the exception of some loose, sharp shale that made my ankles roll. But I should have known by now it couldn't be that easy.

After about 5 miles we noted that the shoreline of the lake had completely disappeared under water. The gates of the local dam had been opened, and the shore on our side AND the opposite side of the lake was no more. While we could have gone back the way we came, it would have been dangerous and probably longer. Great. Ahead we could climb straight up a sheer rock face with no ropes or pitons, or we could climb around the rock a nice extra mile or two.

We began the ascent. Myron took the quick route and climbed the sheer rock that protruded from the lake. The rest of us took the long route up and over the rocks. Or, perhaps I should say, our daughter and Myron's friend climbed while baby-sitting me. I had to stop every five minutes because of sharp pains in my chest. Know why the mountains of Northern California are called the "High Sierras?" They call them "High" because they are. High I mean. And the "higher" you go up on a mountain, the thinner the air. Breathing became an issue for me, being the out-of-shape Blonde Step-mom.

As the temperature rose, and we kept climbing, I ran out of water and food. The temperature outside felt like a rousing 90 something degrees against the bare rocks. My head began to throb from the beginnings of heat stroke. Ahead of us loomed a dark mountain pool, with a slick of green algae around its edges. I noticed a slight movement of the water. Great, it's not stagnant, I thought. Of course the bear track in the mud nearby meant we weren't alone, but at that point bacteria or not, I needed the water. I prayed as I refilled the water bottle and gulped it down. A splash of cool on my face and we were off again. My vision was beginning to blur, and exhaustion had made my body uncooperative on the steep incline.

By this time Myron had rejoined the group and we saw that one major rock hurdle stood between us and the last remaining shoreline back to camp. The barren rock was a round, no handholds, no elevator, Bruce Willis-type climb. (And by now you've probably noticed — I'm not John McClane). It was approximately 300 feet above the tops of the trees below. THAT'S where my prayer whining kicked in.

"Lord, please send a helicopter. I can't make it. Everything hurts, I can't breathe, my head has exploded and I can't climb one more moment. I need to be rescued, please!"

As I slowly trudged up behind the group, I did the one thing that your Daddy always told you not to do while climbing. I looked down. The lake appeared like a large mud puddle off in the distance below us, and the tops of the tall pine trees a jagged bunch of green spears, waiting for me to fall. While the view from the top was breathtaking, I didn't appreciate it much. So, in true cowardly fashion, I froze.

Fear is the opposite of faith. Fear will paralyze you and prevent any forward momentum. I can testify to that because I clutched at the rock and could not move my feet. I didn't cry, just silently prayed for some sort of TV-style rescue.

Then I felt something touch my hand. I looked up and it was my husband's leather belt. He leaned over the edge of the rock, and handed it to me, buckle first. Ok, it wasn't a helicopter, but I was grateful, just the same.

"Grab this," he said. I did, and with great skill, he hauled me up the face of that rock until the terrain leveled off and I could walk without the fear of falling. He watched me closely and saw that I had grown very weak and sick. He spurted ahead of the group, scrambled down the narrow, steep shale shoreline, and pushed a large dead tree onto the edge of the lake. Then he caught back up with us and grabbed my hand. Dana and Jerome resumed the hike on around the lake, not willing to try Myron's new mode of travel.

"We're going back to camp the fast way. We're going swimming!" He nudged me into the water, launched the log, and the next thing I knew we were floating across a very deep lake on a log that was filled with bee nests and whatever else lived in it. I fought to control my fears of the insects and lake snakes or fish or any other monsters that might have lurked in the dark waters.

Somewhere in mid-swim, I noticed that the cold waters of the lake were bringing strength to my body. My head stopped throbbing, and my vision started to clear. About one mile later, we washed up to the shore near camp. Myron had me grab the sharp rocks and he scrambled out of the water, reached down, and pulled me out of the lake.

"There!" He exclaimed with a wry smile, "You've passed your survival training!" I turned around to survey where we had been. The lake was approximately 12 miles long, surrounded by steep rocks, and we had hiked the length of it in searing heat, while drinking untreated lake water. I had indeed lived through the valley of the shadow. Joy flooded over me. We had overcome yet again. And suddenly, I felt great. Victory was sweet, if a bit tiring. A kind of death to life experience.

But I definitely need more faith to pass signs that say "No Cars."

Always move forward and don't look back. Like the flooded stream and the long hike, you always went forward and came out ok. It's when humans give up and try to go back to old habits that they end up in trouble. It does take faith to move forward. Sometimes you have to just do it.

CHAPTER 37

India

MY FRIEND LORELEI called me up to invite me on a mission trip to Northern India. I had difficulty containing my excitement, as we were promised all sorts of exciting times: miracles, getting to know the people, visits to villages, and even a trip to a leper colony.

Originally we had planned to leave in September. An unexpected delay occurred that pushed the trip a week later. Good thing, too. The train we would have taken to the leper colony was blown up by terrorists — we would have been on that train had we gone at the original date. It was only the first in a series of near-misses that proved to me that God takes good care of His kids.

The flights were long and exhausting. The trips through foreign airports and different customs counters seemed to take forever. 36 hours after we started, we landed in New Delhi, India.

The air was a foul smelling smog-filled fright. I was somewhat disoriented from lack of sleep. Confusion seemed to be the order of the day in that city. People were yelling and flailing their arms around. They couldn't make simple decisions like whether to back the bus up or go forward when the road was too narrow. We decided to make the final block a walking trip when our bus driver and every person standing on the side of the road started yelling at each other. All he had to do was back up and go around the block. Apparently that was beyond any idea put forward at the time.

Our local host handed out special clothing for us ladies to wear. Some places we could wear American clothes, but not in the villages. We needed to cover our heads there and wear native dress. Pants with long tunics and headscarves. Mine was the perfect color: copper to match my hair.

Elephants were loose in the back yard of the hotel. Monkeys ran around the buildings. Cows wandered the streets. Since the cows were sacred to Hindus—they took a dim view of anyone touching or harming a cow. All the animals were skinny with their bones sticking out. The dogs had mange. The donkeys were overloaded with huge piles of hay hanging off the sides. They could hardly move at all. If animals were so sacred there, why were they treated so badly?

Streets were also filled with human waste and animal feces. It was no wonder the mosquitoes carried fevers there. Somehow it didn't match the stark white and deep blue of the travel brochures. Someone with a photo shop transformed India from filthy to lovely. The rivers were almost black with pollution. There was deep greenish foam on the Ganges River. We were heavily admonished to stay with the bottled water given to us by the hosts and not venture to the vendors on the street. Contaminated water could kill us.

People lived in garbage piles in India. Children hollowed out holes in the garbage dump and lived inside. They ate from the garbage too. My heart broke for them. As we drove by those garbage houses, we realized that so many millions of people would never be freed from such grinding poverty. There wasn't enough money in the entire world to take care of them all.

The bus drove to the northern countryside, a 12 hour ride. We arrived in Amritsar, Northern India, not far from Pakistan. There were armed guards at check points along the road. We suddenly realized that this was a serious trip, and not necessarily safe.

One stop was a village named Rai Chek. Water buffalo roamed the streets. The sewer was an open trench that surrounded the houses. And the bathroom was a trip to the brush. Where the cobras roam. Not my favorite animals.

We took off our shoes and sat on the floor mats inside the little adobe church. I played the keyboard for worship on battery power. 12 year old Preeti sang with me. She was the daughter of our host, and was hopeful that she would become a doctor when she grew up. What a joy it was to sing with her songs that are known the world over.

The people were excited that we had come. Some ladies had fevers, and we had no idea whether they suffered from Malaria, Dengue Fever, or some other malady. We hugged them anyway. They were desperate for love. After the services, the whole village walked back out to the road with us, and the water buffalo followed like big dogs. Very big dogs. With horns.

The people gave us all necklaces of red and yellow tinsel, and clung to us as if they did not want us to leave. What precious Believers, and what a special memory that time engraved in my heart. I only wish I had known what was ahead. I might have asked to stay in the village with no bathroom.

We drove to a local pastor's house near Amritsar to have a small service. He had a water buffalo of his own and kept it on his front porch. He also had a monkey. The monkey was a little hyper. But the animals were well cared for, not like the ones that were running loose.

I played the keyboard again. The local pastor asked me to pray for a little boy who was demon-possessed. I was not on the prayer team. I was not supposed to do any ministry while we were in India. He insisted. I prayed for the boy and his eyes changed to a dark brown—with a twinkle! He smiled and waved his arms. The dad remarked that he hadn't smiled for months.

I was very excited!

It was time to leave and pack up the keyboard. As I exited the home, everything started going gray. In an instant I shouted "Help!" and passed out on the ground.

Abruptly I felt surrounded by a white cloud. It was if I floated in total peace and comfort. I had the general sensation that I was dying, but didn't really care very much.

Then I heard someone calling to me. I heard the words, "I command you to live in the Name of Jesus!"

I woke up. Lorelei and our Indian host were sitting beside me. They had carried me back to the bus and started to pray. They said my lips were blue and my eyes were rolled back in my head. I remember nothing but the white cloud. Another death to life experience. Literally. Remind me not to get cocky about praying over someone ever again, ok?

We returned to New Delhi for the last healing services. We were not allowed call them crusades there because of the history with the Crusaders who wiped out whole communities of "pagans."

Word came of an explosion at the marketplace where we were going shopping in the next few days. If it was the work of enemies, they weren't very well informed. They missed us.

The local host asked if I would play the keyboard for the services. Our team leader said no. They argued. He worried about me being exposed in case of trouble. After several false trips to the stage, I finally sat down at the keyboard and stayed for the duration. The only danger turned out to be a swarm of mosquitoes. Tough to hide from them. In spite of the repellant, I ended up with a large stack of bites to deal with later.

The prayer lines were incredibly long every night of the trip. People came for healing, and they came straight from the Hindu or Sikh temple. Some still had colored ash on their foreheads from worshiping other gods. God didn't care. He loved them. If they were sick, they were outcasts, and destined to starve in the streets.

So many miracles. Like the cross-eyed boy whose eyes instantly became normal. His father wept with joy. He was a policeman who was sent to arrest us. Instead he saw miracles and came back with his son in tow. He had spent all their money on doctors with no progress. He became a Christian, and shouted "This is the Living God!" into the microphone.

The people surged against the rope. They climbed over the barriers. They wanted the Living God. They wanted life. A crippled boy about 10 years old was lifted into the prayer line. Afterward, he left his wooden crutches leaning against the platform. He came as an outcast; he left with a new lease on life.

One young man lived in the cemetery. He cut himself and screamed every day. His mother brought him to the line for prayer. He fell to the ground, writhing, foaming at the mouth! As the prayer continued, he abruptly stopped writhing and sat up, completely in his right mind! His mother was ecstatic. She had her son back. He hugged her for the first time since he was a child.

A Sikh priest walked through the line for the second time in two days. The night before his tumor had shrunk a little. He asked for more prayer, and as the team laid hands on his stomach, the basketball sized tumor disappeared! He wept with joy and removed his turban. He was ready to serve the only Living God.

After a few days of meetings, we returned to the hotel and packed for the long trip home. On the way to the airport we stopped at a local church service. During testimony time, a man dragged his daughter up to the front of the room while holding on to her finger. The man was a member of a local terrorist group that actively burned down churches and killed believers. He was beating a Christian pastor and burning down his church while his wife took their daughter to our healing service. The daughter had only a partial finger on one hand. God gave her a new finger at the service! He came home, saw her hand, and fell to his knees. He renounced his membership in the terrorist group and joined the local church. That was one of the greatest miracles of all.

As we gave goodbye gifts to the people, and they returned in kind, I realized how blessed I was to live in America. The Indian people are precious and wonderful, their nation interesting and ancient. But my home, my America is where my heart will always be.

In a place where human life hasn't the same value, you got to see God heal the sick and change lives in spite of their situations. Resurrection is a gift. And God gives it to anyone who asks for it. I'm glad your friends prayed you back to life. It's a promise of purpose.

I'm glad too, Red.

CHAPTER 38

Wolves and Warriors

PEOPLE SEEM TO be terrified of wolves. Never mind that the wolf is the foundational species of 99% of all dogs. So somewhere in our history, man and wolf got together and became friends. Hence our experience with a malamute-wolf mix named "Leushen." Some say the name is a variant of "Lucian" which means "light." I'm not sure that's a good description of Leushen's behavior.

He came to us by way of our son Jerry, who fell for him at the dog shelter in Moscow, Idaho. He didn't have a place to keep him, so we became the victims, oops I mean recipients. We figured Joshua the Newfy would love to have a companion anyway, so why not a wolf mix? Two big dogs are always better than one, right?

Joshua was a big house dog. Leushen, on the other hand, was destructo-dog. He was approximately 6 months old when he came to live with us. He had been severely abused and cowered as we reached out to pet him. But he was a beautiful animal with big yellow eyes, grey, red, black, and silver tipped fur. We knew he'd be a work in progress, but we really had no concept.

We were unaware that the wolf breed will eat anything. By anything I mean couches, phone jacks, metal detectors, television remotes, you name it. Finally after numerous attempts to stop him from eating the entire house, even to the use of Tabasco sauce (that just made it taste better), we gave up and put him outside. There he could eat the sprinklers, the hoses, the tulip and iris bulbs, and the neighborhood mice. We were hoping he'd eat a couple of the neighbors too, but no such luck. He looked ferocious, but he was a pussy cat.

Along the way, he launched himself off the back porch on a dead run to bark at some dog somewhere and tore the ligaments in one of his back legs. He couldn't walk without excruciating pain. We packed him up and raced to the vet, who calmly and lovingly explained that either he would be lame for the rest of his life or we could spend $750 on surgery. At that time we did not have $750. So we brought him back with me in tears and left him lying on a sleeping bag in the breezeway.

A couple of days later he managed to re-launch in another barking fit and tear the ligament in his OTHER back leg. Now he was down for the count. His pathetic prone position in the back yard broke my heart. So I prayed. He didn't move for a couple of days. He couldn't even get to the food bowl, so I hand-carried it to him.

After a few days of doggy room service, I looked out the back window and was amazed to find him running behind his pal Joshua across the back lawn! He did not limp, nor did he whelp from pain. He was completely healed. For the rest of his life, which was pretty long for a big dog, he ran and played with his doggy friend with no problems at all.

We learned that shelter dogs sometimes require a little more work than puppies from a breeder, but they can become the best dogs in the world.

When Joshua entered his final battle, it was one that he could not win. In life he had "fit d'battle" for everything from salesmen to marmots, but bone cancer was his match. His death not only devastated me, it shook Leushen to his core. He spent hours panting by my side at night; his head perched on the bed, sorrow and grief filling his big yellow eyes. In order to keep our hearts from breaking, within a few days we purchased a new Newfy puppy named Zeke.

As the new duo grew to become fast friends, there was a distinct difference in Leushen's spirit. He and Joshua had been wise and gentle warriors, loyal to the very end. How we would miss their presence in our pack. The new dog was not any kind of warrior, more of a quiet lover dog. Leushen picked up the torch and became "alpha dog" to teach Zeke the ropes.

When Leushen passed into eternity a few years later, Zeke became inconsolable and often mournfully howled with a deep, gravelly noise that made the neighbors think he had a sore throat. In an effort to help us both survive the loss, we purchased Red Dog from the shelter in Spokane, Washington. And while they got along famously to the point of sleeping curled up together on the dog bed, the personalities and spirit of the new duo was different. Our warriors were gone, their memory firmly ensconced in our hearts. Zeke and Red were the new kinder, gentler duo around our home until Zeke passed away unexpectedly from hemolytic anemia.

Leushen and Zeke with Maddie

Rescuing a shelter dog is a symbol for what God does for people. Death is often the result when animals are not adopted. Without a relationship to God, people are on a collision course with death. When God adopts those who accept Him, He keeps them close to His heart for eternity. I am personally grateful for your love.

You are so very welcome, Red.

CHAPTER 39

Soldiers and Full Circles

JERRY, OUR SON, was due to graduate from Army boot camp in Oklahoma. The whole family was flying down to see him. I'd never been down south, so this promised to be another adventure. Someday I will learn that for the Higbee family, the word "adventure" is more like an Indiana Jones movie.

The motel had a scary, "Psycho"-like atmosphere. We had made reservations at a "Red Lion" only to find that the chain had removed the hotel from their purview because of a lack of proper upkeep. That's an understatement. There were blood stains on the carpet. The toilet seat was black around the edges and didn't fit very well. There was mold on the molding. The place was buggy. All the hotels were full, so there was no way to switch. The town seemed dreadfully run down. Shouldn't it be nicer for the troops? As we pondered the lack of respect for our men and women in uniform, we drove to the auditorium on base for the ceremony.

We have always been very proud of Jerry. Even though he is my step-son, I love him as though he is my very own, and the family has always been willing to "share" him. Jerry's willingness to secure America from her enemies will always be a source of pride and honor in our family. Many men of our family on different sides have faithfully served our nation since the Revolutionary War. Jerry joined the ranks of those who have kept us free as he stepped from civilian life into the US Military. His destiny is a sort of full circle for the entire family.

Jerry and his comrades were quite handsome in their uniforms. The room for the graduation was packed with families from all over the country. Let me rephrase that: there were lots of noisy families there and all were jammed into a tiny auditorium. I couldn't hear what they were saying through the ancient microphone as it echoed and squealed. I only got stepped on a few times while trying to take a photo. Not too bad. Although being a North Idaho like-the-solitude kind of girl I did have to resist the temptation to smack a couple of the more pushy ones that tried to step on me. Don't worry, I was a good girl. Fortunately, afterwards we retired to the restaurant for food. A good meal always brightens my day.

We moseyed around the base and took pictures beside the big tanks and guns. I noted that our granddaughter really liked "Big Bertha" the giant cannon, and had to climb up on it for a pose in her pretty blue dress. This could mean something for her future. I really don't want to know what.

The hotel staff was very nice, if a bit rattled. One in particular was a little over-the-top in demeanor, but sweet. She was a precious Black lady with whom I chatted for a few minutes about a concert or play or something or another that had hit town that weekend. After I sat down in the lobby to wait for the rest of my family after the ceremony, all sorts of mayhem broke loose.

"That there's a prayer warrior, glory to God! Y'all know that there's a prayer warrior. Here, sister, y'all go in the other room and pray!" She pointed at me and bobbed up and down, dragging some poor unsuspecting woman whose family had been in a traffic accident towards me. She ushered us into the dining room behind the lobby. Yikes. I prayed, the lady cried, and it was over in a couple of minutes. So much for being unobtrusive.

We flew out of Oklahoma City on our way home the next day. I rummaged through the SkyWest Magazine from the back of the seat, when something grabbed my attention. It was a story about wild horses! Dan Johnson, a Wyoming photographer, had followed them for years in the same desert as my childhood. My heart pounded with hope. Perhaps he had seen Blackwatch!

I took the magazine home and emailed Mr. Johnson. His answer was tentative. Maybe. He couldn't prove it, but he had seen a black mustang not far from Lander, Wyoming many years ago.

Two weeks later, a package arrived in the mail. Two slide photos of a black stallion standing as a sentinel on the ridge! It looked very much like the Blackwatch I remembered. My wild horse, my symbol of freedom, my guardian of the desert would never be stolen again. A part of my history had been restored. My wild horse and I had completed that "full circle."

Blackwatch, your legacy to me will never be forgotten. I can only pray that your watchful spirit and your wild descendants will prevail through the march of time. You truly are and always will be the quiet song of my heart, my guardian of the desert.

CHAPTER 40

A Doctor in the Family

OUR DAUGHTER DANA graduated from Medical School in Denver, Colorado. The entire family came to Denver to watch her program and celebrate with her friends. She had a new home; though I'm not sure we liked the neighborhood. Hood is the operative word. There was gang graffiti on her garbage dumpster and that made us all nervous.

When we arrived, a press release revealed that Denver squirrels had the plague. Bubonic plague. Dana's trees were full of squirrels. Sigh. Just another thing to worry about.

She had family staying with her that first night, and a malfunctioning bathroom. We "old" people had to climb down her steep basement stairs to use the extra bathroom until the upstairs one was fixed. It was only the beginning of yet another Higbee "adventure."

A friend called up Dana and needed a baby sitter for the night. Dana said ok. The night before graduation, with a house full of people she volunteered to babysit an infant. While we wondered if she had been eating nuts from the squirrel stash, we realized she is a wonderful friend. If Dana is your friend, you have a solid, stable one.

The graduation proceeded the next morning. We all gathered for photos with Dana, the Doctor. We were so very proud of her (and still are, I might add)! The graduation party was supposed to start at 4pm, so we had to go get the supplies.

We arrived back at her house, but she had lost her house keys. The house had been "burglar proofed" so unless we wanted to actually break out windows and hire a 4 year old to crawl through, we were out of luck. So we sat on the back patio and ate chicken. What else do you do when you have to go to the bathroom and you can't do anything else?

Within a space of an hour or so, a friend arrived with her keys—they were stuck in the baby's blanket. So much for babysitting when it's stressful. Dana opened the door.

That's when things got really interesting. The upstairs bathroom was fixed, but now the downstairs toilet had overflowed. The entire bathroom was covered with unthinkables in the shower, on the floor, in the sink. The clock was ticking down toward party time. We had to get it cleaned up by 4pm, and Roto-Rooter needed to be called. It was going to be close. Evelyn, Dana's Mom, and I grabbed the paper towels, disinfectant, cleaners and went for it. It was another Higbee survival training episode.

By 4pm, everything was back to "normal" and the house filled up with family and friends. The celebration began in earnest. Dana would become a great doctor. Good thing. She'd need it. She's a Higbee.

If people would just do what they have to do when disaster strikes, instead of panicking, they'd get through anything. Some people panic and give up. I'm glad this family keeps on going.

Yes, Red. If we don't overcome the obstacles, the obstacles overcome us. And Dr. Dana got married in 2013. She is one beautiful lady, with two children now. And she's still a doctor. Obstacles is an understatement.

CHAPTER 41

A River with No Water

IF YOU ARE not familiar with North Idaho, you're missing spectacular scenery: forests drenched in golden sunlight, snow-tipped craggy peaks, lakes that sparkle like loose diamonds in morning light and all abundantly criss-crossed by rivers. Well, most of the time. Sometimes the beauty of life is obscured by its circumstances. Maybe I can help you with that.

As you have probably guessed by now, our family doesn't have "outings" like most families. So in keeping with the Higbee Survival Training Club, I share this one with you in hopes that it may encourage you. Some of you are probably going through "H.E.double toothpicks" in your personal lives, so just maybe our little incident will gently show you that whatever you're experiencing in your life may in fact hold hope in disguise. And even a little moment or two of humor. It's something to contemplate over a nice hot cup of coffee.

Our son Jerry had been at Fort Meade training to become an officer, and our daughter, Dr. Dana, had come home to Idaho for a short August visit. We didn't know if we'd see any of them at the Holidays, so the family planned a float trip down the Coeur d'Alene River. (You may Google-Earth that if you need to see it for real).

Evelyn and I had almost decided to stay on shore and maybe babysit the dogs, but someone talked us into floating with the entourage. What we forgot was the history of our family outings. Remember the old saying, "Those who forget history are doomed to repeat it?" Yep, that was us.

The day dawned bright and beautiful. After a several week stretch of high 90's, it was only supposed to get to the low 80's that day, so we were very hopeful we wouldn't cook right onto the rubber of the inner tubes. We loaded up with sun block, grabbed our collective hats, covered up the sun sensitive portions of the body and headed out for the fun.

The dogs were mad from the get-go because our plans had changed and they didn't get to go. Turned out they had reason to be perturbed but I'll get back to that later. We figured we'd float the river starting just before noon, have lunch, and get home by 3 or 4 pm.

We picked up our daughter's best friend Jennifer at the Starbucks in Coeur d'Alene, Idaho. You cannot start a family outing without Starbucks; it's bad luck, sort of like the cigar in the movie "Independence Day." Since we women were the only ones there, I can tell you that it was probably the guy's fault the trip had problems. If they'd stopped for a Starbucks, we'd have all been just fine.

We loaded up and headed for Enaville, Idaho. Enaville is also known as the "Snake Pit" for those of you unfamiliar with Shoshone County. The first time I ever heard that reference to the restaurant that serves Rocky Mountain Oysters, it was because of a biker riot that had deputies and troopers and gunfire echoing over my police dispatch microphone in the early 70's. The place had a rep then. It's a pretty decent place to eat now, if you don't mind the name. And, for you who are not familiar with Pacific Northwest cuisine, "Rocky Mountain Oysters" are the testicles of cattle or elk, or whatever else they have on hand to serve. Why, Montana even has a "testicle festival" to celebrate the fare. Ok, ok, go throw up and come back, I promise not to be so graphic in the rest of the story.

Once everyone arrived at the "Snake Pit" parking lot with inner tubes and actual gas in their car, we headed up the river road to find a spot to get into the water. There was water somewhere. Myron and I had floated that river in a boat several times before, but this time it was terribly shallow everywhere we looked. Did I mention North Idaho was in a drought? It's an excellent time to go tubing on a river. Not.

The Coeur d'Alene River winds through a rocky canyon with numerous "special" places that locals use for swimming. We parked at one of those spots, and since it didn't seem very far off the road itself, it looked like a good place to float to at the end of our journey. (Hint: never trust your own judgments concerning what's good or bad, uh, it can be deceiving). Those spots are the deep parts of the river and include jagged rocks that jut into the water, (or swampy mosquito holes with gravel beaches). Then there's the small town of "Prichard", three miles away from where we left the car. A camping spot, swimming hole, restaurant, and bar all rolled into one. Whatta deal!

We failed to realize that 3 miles on a road is not the same as 3 miles on a river. As the Bible would say, "Here is the beginning of wisdom:" a) if you want a short trip, make a short trip, don't add to it; b) if the water is shallow at its deepest point, you're gonna be sorry at its normally shallow points.

We drove 8 miles (yes, I said 8) past Prichard to what appeared to be some very shallow water, and parked at the edge of the road with the other two vehicles. The embankment was steep, especially for those of us who weigh more than some Olympic sprinter, so my sweet husband made a rope for us to use to steady ourselves on the way to the water. We pitched the inner tubes into the water and proceeded to attempt a launch.

Right off the bat we noted that we would probably walk over the slick rocks a lot. The water was only 3 or 4 inches deep in spots, and our weight didn't seem to help the floating part of the experience. My particular rear end hit bottom right off the get-go, so I didn't "get goin'" right away. Jerry had the beer chest on a float tube, and my husband

Myron had some pop in his dive bag, but we were immediately spread so far apart that I'd never catch up to the good refreshments. I was definitely in the wrong place.

By 12:30pm (We started at around 11:05am), most of us were pooped. And we hadn't gone very far. By 3pm I knew exactly what a professional baseball pitcher against a team of chimps felt like his first day on the job: black and blue all over and a shoulder that hurt like crazy.

I did have a sort of refreshment bag of my own—a few plastic Wal-Mart bags (with a Ziploc bag inside) tied to my pants. It carried two bottles of water and some crackers. I quickly discovered that when a plastic bag fills with water, it's much heavier than normal. Uh, and water can pull your pants off. No kidding. I'd have to stand up to walk through the shallows, and my pants would slide down my backside. Now, the river was not deserted that day because it wasn't just our little troop of 9 people on it. I didn't sign up for flashing.

Once I realized my pants were creeping down toward my ankles and I was having difficulty standing to walk over those rocky parts of shallow water, I cut the bag off with fingernail clippers. Where did I get them you ask? Off my keychain which was clipped to the other side of my pants by a carabineer of course. If you've never had one, get one, they are the best invention since sliced bread for not losing your keys on a tubing trip.

Tri-focals are another issue you might put in your travel-awareness folder. Fast moving water and tri-focals are a Murphy's Law exercise waiting to happen. The Coeur d'Alene River may run through the Silver Valley, but when you wear tri-focals it just runs in circles. I had to slide my feet along the bottom until my feet stopped and not look at the water in order to stand up without falling over. I think it said something to me about keeping my spiritual vision clear as well. Life can make you crash and burn just like those slick rocks.

A friend of the family dragged a walking stick off the bank for me, which helped immensely for my balance. No one seemed to mind my wielding that clunky thing except the tiny water snake that slithered out from under my foot in one spot. Poor little guy or gal or whatever. I knew I was getting delirious because I bent over and talked to it.

"Aren't you just the sweetest little thing? Whatcha doin?"

I'm not a big snake lover, but for some reason felt empathy for the tiny black snake with beady eyes. I learned later that our grand daughter had talked to it too, so maybe no one will have me committed to a mental institution yet. See? Trouble can change your whole outlook.

By this time, Jennifer was done with rafting. She had hoped it would be a short trip. Well... she was late to an appointment. Not late, exactly, perhaps absent was a better term. We were nowhere near our car. It's an exercise of faith, you know. Not knowing where you are, where you're going, or if you're ever going to get there. You just know that the river goes one direction and eventually, even if you're a water-logged, shriveled up mess you'll find your way home.

Two of our number had disappeared from the river entirely, and I didn't see them behind me, so I grabbed a rock and waited to see if anyone knew what happened to them. Apparently they got so tired they climbed out of the water and hiked off somewhere. WHERE, exactly no one knew because no one knew where we were either.

I asked my husband where we were and he replied "in the river." Which helped me tremendously. I explained that Jennifer had to leave and I should take her back to the car so she could go home.

He responded with this stunning announcement. "There's a long way to go, and it will take you longer by walking than if we stay in the water." Sigh. Jennifer missed her appointment. And we missed lunch AND dinner.

That little fact really hurt my family, as Jennifer is a very special friend. Dana was bummed and felt guilty about making such a long trip. It wasn't intentional, it was just life. The river of life doesn't always take you where you think you should go, sometimes it takes a detour. You just have to be flexible and enjoy the float, even when you have to walk a bit.

I glanced at my 4 dollar Wal-Mart watch and noted that it was still running just fine. It had been in the river for almost 4 hours and was still working. Wow. I was so fascinated with that fact that I failed to check on Jennifer. Then she hit a rock—smack! A huge boulder had appeared in the middle of the river with nasty current to boot—and her shoe went flying! Of course she was drenched worse than before and now shoeless. Well, someone did recover her shoe eventually, which is a miracle in itself.

Soon everyone re-positioned and we were strung out along the river. Jerry and his fiance Mindy were so far behind us that they were out of sight entirely. Still dragging the cooler down the river, I suspected it was a good thing he was in great physical condition from his military training.

Finally my husband, granddaughter, family friend, and Jennifer disappeared ahead of us, leaving just Dana and I in our section of the wilderness. As we rounded the bend, and avoided a nasty big whirlpool that probably would have sunk me forever, she exclaimed, "I see a trail!"

Oh, Yay, we gotta get outta here, I thought. I tried to stand up, but the water in that spot had a smaller "eddy" moving under the surface. For you non-Idahoans, an "eddy" is a whirlpool current that causes great annoyance to rafters and can make you go in a circle. It can also suck you under the water if you're not very very careful.

A little assistance from Dr. Dana, and I was up on the shore walking down the path. Finally. We navigated through the trail out onto the main road. We recognized the trailer park from earlier in the day, so we knew to turn right and walk towards the Prichard campground.

By 4:30pm we wandered to the camp and met up with our two missing adventurers. It was a huge relief to see their faces after watching the rapids come and go and having no clue where we were. A few minutes of anxious waiting, and the rest of the crew dragged themselves onto the beach.

Dr. Dana volunteered to go get the car a short ways down the road. Well, the word "short" probably wasn't quite correct. It was actually three miles away. So off she went in her flip-flops and after all it was right off the road so nothing could possibly go wrong... that was around 4:30pm.

By 5:50pm and no sign of Dana, we were all extremely worried. Had she fallen? Had someone run over her? Was the car missing? Had some scary North Idaho version of "The Hitchhiker" occurred? We assigned our resident military tough guy, Jerry, to go get her.

By 6:40pm, we were getting ready to bribe some campers to take us to the cars. Some of us were freezing as the temperature slowly cooled off. The rest of us had not eaten since breakfast. I had opened the sack I'd removed from my waist and passed out crackers and beef jerky, but it was wearing off. Jerry had left the cooler with a few refreshments and a bag of nuts, and Myron still had a couple of cokes left. Although I think we were the nuts.

Oh, and are you aware that when your shorts are wet they don't come down easily at the rest room? Just a tip from someone who knows: it might require a little extra work on your part.

We occupied ourselves by playing with empty pop cans full of bees, and watching the road intently for every car that passed us. Our granddaughter Maddie crowned me Queen of Flowers, and her other Grandma The Queen Mother, so that made up for any inconvenience. And before you ask, no one had a cell phone on them and there isn't any service in the tool-dingies anyway. Welcome to North Idaho.

Somewhere just before 7pm-ish, Jerry and Dana drove in to the camp. All that walking and she never found the car until Jerry found her. It was a tad further down the road and OFF the road than we thought. Somehow, things look easier when you're behind the wheel of the car than when you're tired, hungry, and sore. We're just grateful she was ok! I was able to dump the "Hitchhiker" movie scenes out of my mind at that point.

Less than a half hour later, all the vehicles came back and we loaded up to go home. Yes, we were all still hungry, in case you were wondering.

Jennifer sped off to her Mom's after the long tiring day on the river. As soon as cell service was restored Dana called ahead to let her know Jennifer was coming. She still felt bad at her friend's loss of the day, but Jennifer was a trooper and chalked it up to the "living on earth" syndrome.

At this point you're thinking, *they ride off into the sunset and live happily ever-after.* If you think that you don't know this family very well. On the wicked windy road that runs beside the river, Dana suddenly discovered she had forgotten her camera in her brother's car. We also wondered what happened to the food she had purchased the day before the trip. You know, turkey, bread, pickles, chips... oh, it was halfway to our house by now in the back of her Dad's truck. So much for dinner.

So Dana called her brother, and asked him to stop by the Enaville parking lot and drop off her camera, since she was headed back to Denver early the next morning. Probably shouldn't have made it sound that urgent, as Jerry sped up to meet us.

The next thing we knew Jerry had pulled in beside us at Enaville and a police car pulled in right behind him. I asked him what he had done, but he had no clue. Don't worry, the deputy knew. Did I mention it was a wicked windy road? The speed limit is only 45 or 50. Oh, well.

Jerry turned on the military charm and the officer let him go with a "thank you for your service." God bless that guy. It was the perfect ending to a perfect day.

Hey, we saw scenic North Idaho from the river (at least the parts that had water), we saw wildlife (a cute water snake and a couple of deer), and we didn't get eaten by mosquitoes. We were grateful. The river did its job, for the most part, with only a few bruises left as remembrances.

Oh, the perturbed dogs? They didn't get dinner until almost 8:30pm. They had found a coat hanger to rip apart, and a set of deer antlers to chew on for revenge. This is North Idaho, after all.

Of course, and as far as we were concerned, even the pizza guy was starving by the time he delivered to our door.

As far as lessons go, I have noted faith is like a river. If you let it be shallow, then you're going to get bumped and bruised and tired throughout your time on this earth. If you open the gates of God's River in you, let that river flow deep and strong, you will float with purpose and meaning. And you may not avoid all the rocks or the whirlpools, or bruises, but at least there will be water that can carry you forward to your destiny.

And, sorry about the hanger and antler.

> Right on, Red. Oh, and don't float the Coeur d'Alene River during a drought. It's not very bright.

CHAPTER 42
Fiji the Second Time Around

ANOTHER MISSION TRIP to Fiji was planned, this time with a group of people rather than by myself.

We arrived at the slightly more modern terminal in Nadi, with less animals and birds in it. Lots more people there this time. The line at Customs was very long—I didn't like the exposure. We all looked alike in our bright red and gaggy yellow polo shirts with the words "Fiji Explosion" on them. I had a bad feeling about the trip, but couldn't quite figure out why. There were 35 of us, all very visible, and it felt unwise somehow. It could have been because of our experience with 9-11-01, but it still gave me the willies.

We stopped in Nadi for lunch. The locals made a big feast for us, with tables of local vegetables and salads. It was a promise of good fellowship and new friends. Or so we thought.

We all piled into the bus and headed out to Suva and our hotel. Right off the bat we noted there was something wrong with the bus driver. He seemed sick or dizzy, and his eyes were dilated.

The bus started to weave all over the road! It was only a two lane road and we were on the wrong side of it! Amazing how fear will drive people to pray. The driver thought he was fine (as he jerked the steering wheel from right to left, and swerved over the curvy highway). One of the ladies went up to talk to him to keep him awake.

That seemed to help. With her present, he seemed to be paying better attention. It was a long 200 miles, but we arrived safely. The guy needed to get some sleep before ferrying us around again.

We received our room assignments for the hotel. It was a more modern hotel compared to the last time I was there. Actually, it was a "Super 8." For some reason, my senses were on full alert from the beginning. This was not a "Higbee Adventure"—this was a possibly dangerous one.

The first service arrived. The speaker's faces had been on posters all over town several weeks before we arrived. Was that wise? I wondered.

Prior to the first meeting, we were invited to the church of a local pastor for dinner. A beautiful feast was prepared for us, and as they set up the tables, my friend Lorelei and I wandered into the sanctuary. The moment we entered, we nearly fell to the floor and began to pray. A deep groaning sound came from me—something I had never experienced before. I immediately had a vision of two animals: a crocodile and a cobra. When the groaning stopped, I had a strange sense of foreboding that would not leave.

We all filed into the auditorium after a dinner of fresh fish and vegetables. Many of the pastor's wives were excited that we were there. They invited the ladies to speak to them during the week.

The evening began with special processions of male dancers carrying lit candles in the dark and amazing dance numbers. Men and young boys wore gold and white satin costumes and in perfect choreographed rhythm leapt with skill across the stage. We all wished our men in America's churches would dump their macho and dance like that!

The next day we held the special meetings for the pastor's wives. They were so broken, so hopeless. We washed their feet and they began to weep. They were lonely, and it seemed as if they had been forgotten by the church entirely. They were incredibly grateful for the love we showed to them.

The team dressed me in a golden sash and long costume for a short skit about Deborah from the Bible. One of the ladies came to me in tears and said that she had never heard that women could be leaders! They had been told that their place was in the home, and that any sort of leadership was forbidden. Our team had made an impact, one that would probably upset the standard order of things.

At the evening service, we prayed for one woman, and she removed her necklace and placed it on my neck. She had felt as though God didn't listen to women. She thought that the heavens were made "of brass." That night, the Lord touched her heart by giving her the exact prayer through us that she had been praying in secret. Once again, the Lord had heard the hearts of the women, and let them know they were part of His plan on the earth.

There was a strange tension in the air after the service. The local teams shooed us out a back entrance instead of the main doors. We didn't know what was happening, but the expressions on the faces of some of the audience were a source of concern.

The next morning, our leaders called a meeting at the hotel. We learned that one of the pastors that we sent advance money to had stolen our funds for the hotel. We were not paid for the two weeks. We are not paid for the first week. We would have to pool our money in order to stay for a week; then our airplane tickets might have to be changed so that we could go home early. We all pitched in as much as we could. Our team leaders were furious and wanted to cancel the rest of the meetings.

We were incensed. We had trusted a brother and he let us down. Plus, several members of the team had come down with a mysterious illness. Two of them had become deathly ill and would leave the group to go home for treatment.

We decided to stay for the rest of the week, and complete the meetings while the team revamped the schedule to shorten it. Three of us rode to the meeting place for one of the morning services. The speaker was a woman—the auditorium was packed with men and they were extremely unhappy about the situation. They sat with their arms folded and glowered at her through the entire meeting. The atmosphere was thick with anger.

As the speaker completed her sermon, one man was healed of an ear problem during the prayers. He jumped up and down with glee and danced across the stage. But no one came to the stage to greet either him or us, and we were ushered out quickly. It was not the normal response to a miracle.

By the evening meeting, I noticed that the local pastor was not speaking English anymore. I felt extreme tension in the room. People were staring at us. They ushered us out again to a different door. They told us to be quiet and careful. I wondered what that pastor had told the audience.

The next morning we learned that the pastor from the previous night told everyone that **we** had stolen money from the local people, and that we had imposed ourselves on them to steal their food. He had turned his own theft around to blame us!

Our leaders were enraged. After the women's meeting, that evening's service would be our last night there. By then, many more members of the team were ill.

That evening we were brought in as usual to the auditorium. We took our seats and waited to see what happened. We were all on alert just in case violence erupted. Anger was definitely in the air.

Our team leader stepped on to the stage and began to speak. He reminded them about integrity and honor, love and truth. The holiness of God descended on the room. It was difficult to breathe from God's Presence. Truth was exposed, and death could be the result of a failure to confess.

He finished with a challenge to the man who stole the money. The pastor broke and wept —and offered confession of his sin. The other pastors apologized to all of us for the dishonor. The atmosphere immediately lifted and friendship returned!

They were suddenly sad to see us stop the meetings and asked if we would stay. But the money was gone—it had been sent to the pastor's son in America for his living expenses. While there was no excuse for his theft, I realized that poverty was so deep in the church in Fiji that even a pastor would steal to help his family. That's not an excuse, but temptation is a reality throughout the church worldwide.

We returned to the hotel. While we were out, one of the team leaders worked a deal with a nice resort to take us for free for the last week in exchange for Christian services. It was a complete miracle! We would stay at an expensive resort for the last week. It was well-deserved relief. While I was still a little apprehensive in my "gut instinct," it seemed like a wonderful blessing after what we had been through. The next day we waved goodbye, hugged the people one last time, and drove off to the resort. We thought it was a sort of vacation. Yep, famous last words again.

The resort literally appeared to sparkle in the Fijian sun. The "cabins" were South Pacific style thatched bungalows that would have normally cost around $450US per night. The resort contained a fancy restaurant with Native motifs, a magnificent ocean view, and an exquisite pool complete with recliners. We were in "hog's heaven."

At least until the first night. My roommate Lorelei and I slept like babies. By morning, we heard that several members of the team had frightening experiences. Some of them had awakened not being able to breathe, as if they were being suffocated. We also learned from the hotel staff that the row of bungalows was situated directly on the path to a firewalker pit. There were forces at work beyond our natural senses.

Another roommate was added to our room. As we rested, she appeared to be sleeping, then awakened and began thrashing around her bed. We leaned over her, but she did not speak. Lorelei sensed that it was not a dream and we began to pray. Within seconds, whatever was causing the young woman's discomfort broke and she was able to communicate. She, too, was unable to breathe. Something had literally made her feel as though a hand were constricting her windpipe. It was then that we realized it was a serious situation.

One morning, after our devotions and a couple of songs, we were accosted by a stranger at our door step. She and her daughter told us they were Christians and had heard us singing. They "just wanted to fellowship and ask for prayer." They were invited inside, but I noted something odd about the daughter. Her eyes were extremely dilated, and no iris was showing.

Lorelei and others prayed over the mother; I only half listened to them. My focus was on the daughter. My red flags were flying and suspicion was growing. The mother spoke about her brother in law who was a drug addict, and babbled on about her bad relationship to the daughter. While they listened, the daughter began to scan the room and pick up things left lying around the tables. She picked up our room keys and started to put them in her pocket. I grabbed her wrist and forced her to put them back.

Her mother yelled at her at that moment in Fijian, so I knew she was well aware of her daughter's actions in spite of the "prayer ministry" going on. As they continued and the woman began to weep, her daughter once again started to pick up items around the room and try to stuff them in her pockets. Once again I stopped her and forced her to return them to the tables. She stared at me with a completely lifeless glare. Well, not totally lifeless, anger seethed under the surface.

By the end of the prayer session the women left, promising to return for lunch the next day. As soon as they were gone, I explained to the ladies in our room that it was a scam. The daughter was under the influence of some type of drug, and the woman was the "ring leader." Needless to say, we notified the resort security staff, and they vowed to protect the patrons from her in the future. She did not return the next day.

A word to the wise: whether you are visiting foreign countries, or a new city in America, be aware of people claiming to be a familiar friend. Not everyone is who they claim to be.

All in all, Fiji was a wonderful blessing for most of us. My friend Lorelei and I had no serious consequences, whereas other members of the team were ill for months afterward. We kept our wits about us and were able to enjoy the precious people of Fiji. We saw many healings and miracles, and watched as God protected us from the plans of those who had other agendas.

There are spiritual realities that humans can't see that play a part in what is going on around us. Atoms, for example make up all matter, yet you can't see them with the naked eye. Flames or lightning also are made up of ionized particles that manifest visibly, but are made of up things not seen. There are spirits that can influence people — just because you can't see them doesn't mean they are not there. Glad you and your friend were paying attention to details. Staying safe in today's dangerous travel environment requires alertness. So if you are going to visit any country that might have a hostile faction, prepare, practice, train, and find a bucket load of wisdom before you go.

You're right Red. What is unseen influences what is seen.

CHAPTER 43

Goodbye, Dad

MY FATHER WAS not big on ceremony. His heroes were John Wayne and Ronald Reagan. And if you didn't like those two people, you might want to run swiftly in the opposite direction. Remember that shotgun?

Dad also was almost as big a practical joker as Mom. One night he ran through our Campfire Girls campout with his shotgun shouting, "Where's that bear? Did you see it?" Not many of my friends slept well that night. Dad got a kick out of it.

He was black and white about people, if he loved you it was forever, and if not … just stay away from him. He loved a variety of folks, from gang bikers that liked his rocks to the Hispanic farm workers that gleaned his apricot orchards. He could read people well, and no one ever messed with him, in spite of what kind of life they might lead.

His last years were spent in Rufus, Oregon running a museum and rock shop along the Columbia River. It was an extensive collection from his past and that of us kids—everything from gem spheres to jewelry, arrowheads and Native American petroglyphs that were salvaged from a dynamite blast. His history of finding rare agates and jade was displayed in cases full of amazing colors—red, black, green, white, pink, and blue. He loved the opportunity to share his knowledge of geology and Native artifacts with school children and rockhounds. The walls of his workshop were lined with hand drawn thank you notes from children all over Oregon. He always passed out a free stone or two to the kids. He was a softy for children, always hoping they would love gems as much as he.

Dad could walk into a rock pit full of gemstone enthusiasts and within five minutes all of them were clustered around him like the Pied Piper. He understood where the best agates were and people could tell immediately. He was always willing to share that knowledge, even if it meant giving away secrets that would have given him the best rocks. Dad had integrity.

At 90 years old he developed severe congestive heart failure. He limped along on crutches and refused to quit, being the active outdoorsy sort until his dying day. He might have slowed down some, but giving up was not in his blood.

To say that he made a name for himself over the course of his life was probably an understatement. One day while my friend Shirley and her husband Steve were visiting a local rockhound club, someone mentioned the name Howard Dolph. She remarked that she had known him and even went rock hunting with him as a kid. That created quite a stir. She finally had her sister Nancy manufacture a t-shirt that read "Yes, I knew Howard Dolph." He would have laughed with joy over that one.

In May of 2004, it became apparent that he was not going to live much longer. As he came close to leaving this earth, a deep sense of loss started to take hold in my heart. He was the rock of the family—the strong one, the invincible bulwark against whatever happened to us all.

The day before he died I spoke to him on the phone and reminded him that God loved him deeply. He grunted. It was pretty funny, that grunt. It wasn't a rejection grunt, it was a "yeah, yeah, yeah I know" grunt. (Didn't know I could understand grunt language, did you?)

The very next morning as I stood at the kitchen sink, these words literally rippled through my heart:

"Today is the day I have waited for all of his life, the day when he will come Home to Me."

That night, Dad passed into eternity.

There are no words for how much I still miss him, all these years later. But I know without doubt that God waited excitedly for his entrance to Heaven, and that he was greeted by the Lord.

Everyone worries about the fate of their loved ones. Yet God thinks on them throughout their lives. He knows the day and the hour when they are due in Heaven. There is no soul too far from God that He cannot redeem.

Preach it, Red.

CHAPTER 44
The Call

OVER THE YEARS, many well-meaning ministers had spoken to me about becoming a pastor, including that Catholic Nun from Fiji. One precious friend, an African Archbishop named Victor Onuigbo, often pointed to me and hollered across the room that I was a pastor. I always assumed he'd been sniffing too much coffee. Others told me they were certain I was to be a pastor, that it was my calling. One minister once told me that I was to "feed the prophets like the ravens fed Elijah." Uh,huh. Weirdo.

The day after the weird raven speech, I dropped by our local grocery store. A loaded grocery cart later, I wheeled my way toward the car. Not that I could really see much of the car. It was literally covered with ravens. And the closer I got to them, the less they moved away. They just stared at me. One bird in particular blocked my passage to the door with a strut and loud cawing. In reality I think he wanted some bread or other tidbit, but spiritually, it was a hint, a hint that I ignored for many years.

One weekend, my friends and I drove to Marysville, Washington for a conference. I looked forward to a few services in which I could just sit around and listen instead of working my tail off. The last day I woke up and took my shower, then sat by the bed while my roommate Flo took hers. She stepped into the bathroom, shut the door, and whack! I fell face first onto the floor of the hotel room and could not move. No, I wasn't sick; it was the Lord's way of getting my attention.

It felt as if I was lying on a beach by the ocean, a strong yet gentle wind blowing over me. The Presence of the Lord wafted around me and over me, quietly whispering both love, and commands that I could not ignore. It was time to start a church. I had been ordained for several years and did nothing. It was His time to follow through with the Call.

When Flo opened the bathroom door, she fell to the floor herself and could not move. One of our friends in the room next door walked into the room and also fell to the floor. We were stuck on the carpet for about an hour until God released us. It was a marvelous, exciting morning. When we were finally able to move, I opened my Bible to a passage about building the house of God. As soon as I arrived home after the conference, a friend had sent me an email with that very same Scripture and told me that God had expressed to him that I should start a church.

The very idea of it scared me spitless. The responsibility, the problems, the hassles did not appeal to me. But it was very clear that God expected me to do it, so in spite of the trepidation, Raven Ministries was born. Notice that I remembered that bird hint from previous years.

Many humans run from God's call on their lives. "Many are called, few are chosen" the Bible says. It's because people prefer to do their own thing. God really calls everyone, but only a few respond.

CHAPTER 45

Reconciliation

I PROMISED RED THAT I would let you know what happened to those friends who moved away and enraged my heart. There were a lot of lessons in that incident, not the least of which was that bitterness can kill you.

It tried to kill me. For about five long years I held anger over the friendships lost from that situation. While I functioned ok on the outside, on the inside I was still seething. Migraines and stomach problems increased. Though I managed to not share any of the gory details of what happened, my heart was not fully recovered from the years of watching my church and friendships dissolve.

One day I received a note in the mail from my former pastor. In it he repented of hurting all of us in the church, and told me that his newest marriage had dissolved. The grief, the sorrow in his letter broke my heart again. All of the rage fell away in that moment, when I realized that he had suffered too, as had his new wife. They simply couldn't work it out. Their pain was evident, as was the terrible devastation that comes from failure to hear the Lord.

It was also a wake-up call about ministry—the pedestals that people erect for their leaders are high and emotional. If we violate them, people get hurt. In one moment of compassion for an old friend, the relationship was restored fully. As I flushed all of my anger and bitterness, our friendship was back on track. Today we are fast friends again in spite of the miles between us, and his life has been strengthened deeply in the Lord. Restoration is a precious gift.

Years later I was asked to attend a Christian meeting. As I entered the sanctuary of the church, a glance at the crowd caused me to take a second look. It was the woman that I had spent so many years hating!

I got up out of my seat, walked over to her, and hugged her. She was a tad apprehensive, but we stood and chatted. Inside my own heart, there was no negative reaction at all. No animosity reared its ugly head, no anger roamed through my thoughts, only joy at seeing a woman who at one time was my friend. God had performed a miracle of reconciliation.

God washed all of the past away with His love.

If only mankind would learn the power of letting go of the past and embracing love. There are only two things God requires: loving Him, and loving each other. If they would do that, the world would not be filled with hatred.

Red, I wish people would listen to you more often.

CHAPTER 46

Farewell to Police Work

WITH THE DEATH of my father in 2004, and after working past my retirement system's points by a year, it seemed the perfect time to leave the job I had held since college. While I looked forward to a new chapter in my life, it also frightened me a bit to lose my law enforcement "identity."

When you are part of law enforcement for 31 years plus change, the camaraderie, the common purpose brings a sense of family (even at the times when it's dysfunctional). I loved the officers, I loved making a difference in my community, and I adored the ladies who worked with me. We didn't always get along or agree with each other, but they were a part of my life I was sad to see go. And I knew the adrenalin rush of excitement would be sorely missed.

I remembered the many situations over the years in which the department struggled to pull together after horrific incidents. One year a police officer from another department was brutally murdered in the parking lot of her own office. We built a newer, very secure police building in hopes of preventing such tragedies. We all lived through the terrible images of September 11, 2001, when hundreds of our compatriots in New York died trying to save innocent lives. We survived when one of our male officers transformed himself into a woman. While that was traumatic for the coworkers who knew him, it was simply another bump in the road that required us to buck up and keep going. Good times and bad ones, we had to do it together—both officers and civilian staff.

After I turned in my resignation, one of my supervisors called me to his office. He and the Captain spent about a half an hour yelling at me, explaining what a bitch I was to them over the years. Shocked and broken to the core, I stood up and walked back to my own office and burst into tears. I had given the job my all, expected excellence from the people around me, and somehow managed to alienate a few of the people I loved the most. Sometimes you can be right and be wrong at the same time. I had missed the signs of anger and resentment.

The last few weeks wore on my heart. One detective and I tangled so strongly that he verbally accosted me with near rage. He flatly told me I didn't know what I was doing and refused to prepare his work according to the guidelines set. It was readily apparent that I no longer had any say in paperwork or guidelines. Leaving meant pulling the plug on every piece of expertise I had given over the years. A few of them were mad and they weren't going to take it anymore.

I finally turned in a request for a few final weeks of vacation, just to remove myself from the emotional drain of it. My retirement party almost started a few fights, as people whom I had cared for over the years dropped by to bid me adieu. Unfortunately, within the ranks of law enforcement, grudges are often beneath the surface. While no actual fist fights broke out among the attendees, the tension was absolutely tangible. I had always tried to work with everyone equally. Too bad others didn't have that ability.

My former neighbor had become a friend. He had honored me as his employee, even promoted me to a supervisory position, and never gave me any reason to pull out the metal lunch pail during his term as

Chief. His predecessors and successors alike helped me learn how to work with anyone through differing personalities.

Weathering different police chiefs, fending off city mayors and administrators who had no clue about how courts and cops needed to work, helping desperate citizens who had been through horrific circumstances, and working with some of the best men and women on earth is now part of my own personal history. The vast majority of my former coworkers were sad to see me go, and still on occasion remark that they miss me. Those are precious comments, ones that I will value always.

One note card from a previous Chief contained a sentence that I will treasure the rest of my life. It also may have been the reason for last minute animosity from a handful of officers.

"Thank you for all you have done for this department. I always noted that you seemed to have more power and knowledge than most of the line supervisors."

Yikes, no wonder.

Three short months after I retired, a new officer on our department, who happened to be a shirt tail relative of mine, was shot during a domestic dispute. The miracle is that he survived, and due to community support, his family was able to function. Permanently disabled, he will never serve as a police officer again. And in 2015, Sgt Greg Moore, whom I worked with for about 5 years, was killed in the line of duty. They are reminders that our police officers deserve our prayers and support.

Today I keep in touch with a few of my former coworkers, including the retired ones. They are still precious to me, and I support their work. To wear a badge and uniform is to become a target. To wear it with integrity of the heart is to serve the people of any community with honor. The police men and women that I have known over the years will always hold a place of respect in my heart.

Respect, courage, strength, and faith, all work together when people are charged with public safety. Grudges can only harm the process, and make teamwork difficult. I hope those men and women will learn how to forgive and walk forward, leaving the past where it belongs. If all of mankind would live in the principle of forgiveness, the world would be a much better place.

Red, I tell ya, you are one awesome animal!

CHAPTER 47
Family Dynamics

FAMILIES SHOULD BE safe, fun places where people not only get along well, but love to do things together. Close friends should be part of the family as well—and that especially includes church families. If we can't be friends with each other, we can't be friends of God.

The fawning, pedestal worshiping, empire building folks in the standard church are missing out on the best part of Christianity: a family of friends. They are not perfect folks, of course. Everyone has their little quirks. In fact I have one friend who told me she loves me because I am "quirky." That's probably a polite term. You can tell by the running conversation with my dog in this book that quirky is probably an understatement.

We work to make our family a place of fun and peace. We welcome the kid's friends as part of the family, and our neighbors and church folks are always welcome. But there is a price—they must put up with our quirky-ness.

My husband, for example is a former logger. After 15 years in the timber industry, a tree smacked into his back and broke some vertebra. Many surgeries and therapy later, he has no ill effects from the ordeal.

He worked for many years as an advocate for the elderly in a social work setting—somewhat different from the woods. I appreciate not having to worry about his life being snuffed by a tree. But on occasion, he scares the living daylights out of me by climbing some of them to trim or whatever he has in his crazy mind. Every Christmas Myron the lumberjack scales one of our spindly little pine trees so that he can hang Christmas lights. Sigh. I take stress vitamins, by the way.

Or there was the time a friend mentioned something about a tree that might fall on his roof, so Myron offered to cut it down right then. The saw roared and the tree fell with perfect accuracy away from the roof. It was amazing. Took a few days for my nails to grow back after I bit them off, but it all worked out fine.

One day a tree crashed onto the main road in front of our house and took all the power lines with it. Live power lines. The emergency services folks stood around trying to figure out what to do while traffic backed up in both directions, leaving a dangerous situation. All the while a sparking power line danced across the road. What did my husband do? Well first he used a stick to move the power line off the middle of the road. Then he took his chain saw and cut the tree up. I'm not sure you are supposed to do that, but it got things moving more quickly. Government has a tendency to be slow in times of need.

He and his childhood friend Jerome are intrepid huckleberry hunters as well. Every summer they spend weeks tramping up steep forest hills in search of the delectable berries. They have shared their hunting sites with bears and never been in any kind of trouble. Myron still has a way with animals, apparently.

Myron is simply fearless, a quality I love in him, even if it does make a little nervous on occasion. That's what faith is for, you know.

Then there's Dana, the doctor, who is also "quirky." One summer, we stopped off at Dillon's Beach in Northern California for a night of camping. It was a cow pasture by the ocean, by the way. No amenities, just a honey bucket perched on the sand in between cow pies. When we awakened the next morning our breakfast included French bread that had passed into fossilization. I skipped that tasty treat, but Dana thought maybe the big cow standing by the picnic table would like it. Not so much. No stale bread for that bovine princess, she wanted real food. As Dana reached toward it, the cow sniffed, lowered its head, and shoved her forward with a loud "mooooo!"

For years afterward we gave her cow reminders. You know, cow calendars, cow coffee cups, cow towels, cow creamers that moo'ed, even a cow cookie jar. Everything we could to remind her of her love-hate relationship with cows. Then she met up with sheep.

One Christmas vacation she volunteered to sheep-sit for some friends. She was unaware that sheep were not humans, as their outlook on life is shall we say, a tad more primeval. After a few head butts and a lot of ram stare downs, she decided that sheep were as dumb as a post and she didn't like them either. Livestock is apparently not her forte.

Dana is lovely, highly intelligent, extremely stable and competent. Her brother, 1st Lieutenant Jerry, is also handsome, stable, intelligent, and highly competent. Both can be quite humorous, just like their Dad. Dana came home to visit once with moose ears on her head. That was before all the security gauntlets currently required.

And we only recently learned that Jerry did some strange antics while courting his wife Mindy. Ask him now and you will get a resounding "no way." That's right, be weird then deny everything!

Just like his Dad. Myron skipped along the road singing frequently while we were courting. Now he sings those crazy songs with our friend Stormy, who also has a large repertoire of goofball music. And they often do it in the middle of church. Who says you can't laugh in church?

All in all, this family enjoys laughter and tries very hard to live life without too much panic. When the inevitable problems occur, we try to help each other over the humps. For me, it's another full circle deal. From a life filled with problems, to a life that overcomes them is a gift for which I will forever be thankful.

CHAPTER 48
The Gift

S NOW POURED OUT of the sky in near blizzard like conditions. The roads were solid ice with several inches of snow on top, and I had to drive to a writer's meeting. I wanted to stay home wrapped in a nice warm 'blankey' with a cup of hot chocolate, but no, there I was driving like "Grandma Moses" down the freeway. The pickup was malfunctioning, and had some sort of thingamajig clunking every time I tried to go faster than 30 mph. Nerve-wracking.

I arrived safely, and after the meeting once again braved the elements, now a nasty curtain of rain-ice dumping from the clouds. Got home safely without cracking the enamel on my teeth, but wasn't going out anymore that day. Never say never.

Two and a half hours later, my husband walked through the door and clutched at his chest. The agony in his voice told me it probably wasn't "gas." His usual "it's starting to abate" remark fell on deaf ears and I practically shoved him out the door. We were going to the hospital in spite of that male genetic defect about not going to the doctor. He listened. Thank God.

The roads were still hair-raising, and the truck was working even less efficiently, but I once again clenched my teeth, prayed my fool head off, and kept pedal to the metal to the hospital. I dumped him off at the entrance and went to park the pickup.

By the time I entered the emergency area, they had him packaged and hooked up in the back room. They were on it like lightning. Not a moment was wasted.

After numerous tests and drugs, they called for the cardiac team. An unseen enemy was trying to take his life, so the hospital jumped into rescue mode.

While they put a stent in one of his arteries, I sat alone in a waiting area. One of the nurses (her name was "Bobbi") sweetly asked if I'd like a cup of tea. She brought my favorite mint mixture and chatted about nonsense for a minute to put me at ease. People have no clue how important nurses are to the universe.

After a while, Dr. Dana called the hospital to get the skinny on her Dad. They fell all over themselves to give her up to date information. And since they spoke doctor and not real English, I only understood about five words of it. But the cardiac doctor, a Dr. Kadel, did come in and give me the low down in normal talk. Bless that guy. He must have been used to frazzled family members.

Bobbi told me she thought I was handling the situation well. Yes, I can put on a nice calm front in an emergency. I was trained to do that. I can keep everything on the outside working while the inside turns to mush. I hadn't eaten lunch, so the blood sugar level was in the basement. I may have looked ok, but fainting was a real possibility. But above all the inside things, my heart and mind had peace. I knew that he would be fine. The love of my life would be with me for a while longer.

They kept him overnight, so I drove home with the truck still thunking, and prayed that it would get me there without having to walk alone in the freezing cold on a dark night. It did. My friend Allison made me a hamburger the minute I walked through the door, as she noted that my face was even whiter than usual.

Friendship, love, God's faithfulness, all of the things that have been spoken of in this book came into play that day. While I administer an international prayer network, there was no way to get that information out for prayer until the next day. My family took care of it for me. They passed the word around and prayer was ascending to heaven on our behalf even though I had no knowledge of it. While I was clenching my teeth, God was already taking care of our needs.

The next day we learned that the seeds of friendship and love sown into the neighborhood had grown a harvest of help. Nearly every one of them called me to let us know that they were there for us if needed.

Life is a gift, and it's not guaranteed while living on the earth. You never know what can happen in any given day. Just have to keep your faith intact as you go.

SECTION 7
Bobby Used-to-be Convict

CHAPTER 49
Drug Kingpin

IN JANUARY OF 2011, I ended up as President of the local Idaho Writer's League. The very first evening meeting, a gentleman walked in and sat down quietly in the back. After the meeting, as usual, I initiated a conversation with him. He handed me a few papers and told me he'd like to hire a "ghost writer" to author a book about his life as a drug kingpin. I glanced at the papers and told him I'd "put it in the IWL newsletter."

The paper never made it to the newsletter, by the way.

That night I read the papers closely as shivers crept up my back. It had my name on it, of that I am convinced. A few years before that, there was an advertisement on Craigslist for someone to be a ghost writer for a drug kingpin. I had been poised to answer that ad, but my husband stopped me.

"No you're not going to write for a drug kingpin. No. No. No."

So much for writing for a drug guy.

Perusing the paper, that ad came to mind. His name was Bobby Wilhelm. I KNEW he had been a drug kingpin, as I filled out his criminal record on numerous occasions, but had never actually met him in person. We also grew up in the same town, had some mutual friends, and went to the same schools.

Who else should write his story but me? Nobody. So I called him up the next day and told him I'd like to give it a shot.

My exceedingly skeptical husband and I met Bobby at his bar … yes he is a bar owner, and also worked at a car dealership at the time. He was on lifetime parole, but who's counting? He tested me with an assignment to see if I was going to be the one to write for him. I passed, and the adventure began.

For the next two years, life … well … entered the twilight zone. The first 6 months or so I just took notes and talked to him about his life. He told me he wanted to write the book, so I started pushing on him … hard. He really didn't want a "ghost writer," he wanted someone to help him get the job done. Of course for someone with the attention span of a tsetse fly, getting the job done was not easy. But we did it together.

CHAPTER 50

Brain Bleed

WE HAD ONE really good chapter under our belts when one morning I woke up had difficulty talking. Nobody noticed it at first, as I took some nice thick steaks out of the freezer in preparation for that night's celebration of our son's return from Iraq. But when our daughter Dana called, she heard something wrong in my speech and called her Mom to take me to the hospital immediately. Just because I only had a vocabulary of two words and one of them was "aphasia," what was the big deal? Evelyn dragged me off to the hospital where they diagnosed me with a brain bleed.

It was only a short setback, as after 4 days in the medical jail house, I immediately started writing again. It literally forced new pathways to form around the scar tissue. It was probably the most expensive "vacation" I've ever had in my life. The word "aphasia" came from watching "Criminal Minds" a lot. Who says television is bad for you?

So after the effects of having my speech messed up stopped, things got back to normal. Oh, and the other word? "Jesus." And I wasn't swearing either.

CHAPTER 51

Adult Supervision

SINCE I INSISTED on my name being on the front cover of his book, Bobby had me put "Adult Supervision" by Faye Higbee. Yes, it was sort of like that.

I interviewed ex-cons, 'still' cons, police officers, Bobby's old girlfriends, drug task force members, friends, relatives, prostitutes, and everyone else he asked me to talk with, all 97 of them. Most of the police weren't sure he had changed, although one State Police officer, Terry Morgan, believed in him enough to help him get a great paying job.

Many of his family were skeptical, but hopeful.

Most of the former drug users knew he had changed. With some, Bobby Wilhelm still had enough of a reputation that I was never in any danger. They were still scared of him. Yippee!

I hugged a prostitute whose sister was murdered by the Spokane Serial Killer Robert Yates. It was never clear if he actually knew that they were twins, and he may have killed the wrong sister. She wept when I hugged her, and I wondered how long it had been since someone touched her with kindness instead of intent. That happened a few times with former drug addicts as well.

I corresponded with the serial killer in prison. His psychopathic tendencies were still evident, even though he had given his life to Jesus. But he decided he loved the book. What does it mean when a serial killer says your book is the best he's ever read? Shudder.

I interviewed a former member of a vicious biker gang, a man whom Bobby absolutely drummed into me that I should be careful what I said to him because he was "dangerous." OK. He wasn't as dangerous the day I went to talk with him. He was on crutches after hurting himself. I asked if I could pray for him afterward (sorry, Bobby) and he also leaked a few tears. You just never know how much a really scary person might be hurting on the inside.

I talked to drug dealers who once worked with my favorite former kingpin, some of whom were not interested in Bobby's book because they were still "in the game." None of them were ever mean to me ... flakey sometimes, but never mean. Yes, they were still scared of Bobby. Thank goodness.

We published the book "Bobby Convict, School of Hard Knocks" in November of 2012 under the Bitterroot Mountain Publishing House imprint. It was a long two years, with ups and downs but few real clashes.

Over these years I have watched this once harsh man grow into a kind hearted person. I watched him go from being not too fond of dogs to having 2 adult dogs with puppies that he dearly loves. He went into real estate and now has licenses in two different states, Idaho and Washington. The parole board let him off lifetime parole (that NEVER happens). He even got a passport (that NEVER happens either). He did all that with a 16 year felony prison record. He has truly changed his life and is thriving as a solid member of the community. He still has a weird sense of humor, but hey, nobody's perfect.

And besides, it's fun to have one of his friends, an ex-Mafia guy, send me happy birthday messages on Facebook. (Sent the Mafia the book. They liked it. Good thing).

Red's adoption of Bobby Convict as his own

I'm especially glad that he is growing as a human. I've heard those drug task force guys say good things about him now. They are amazed and it's good to know that humans can change. You can't judge a drug dealer by his past, and assuming people are always going to be bad isn't wise.

I miss you, Red Dog.

SECTION 8

Uncle Sam's Misguided Children

CHAPTER 52
Curve Ball

2013 ROLLED AROUND, and life threw me a giant, ok humongous, curve ball. I began writing news stories for a Marine veteran owned group called "Uncle Sam's Misguided Children." For the uninitiated, that's the nickname for the United States Marine Corps—U.S.M.C.—and they are truly misguided at times. Other times they are sharp as the blade on a Mameluke sword*. And they can be hilarious. Or not.

---

* The Mameluke sword was given to Lt Presley O'Bannon by Ottoman Empire Viceroy Prince Hamet as a gesture of respect after the US Marine victory at the Battle of Derna in 1805. The cross-hilt swords/sabres are a tradition in the Corps.

Rick Ferran, "Tank" and Tank Jr

CHAPTER 53

Tank, Communism Survivor, Marine Veteran, Misguided Child

MY FRIEND TANK (Rick Ferran) was intimidating at first. In particular, he once didn't understand my colloquial manner of writing and instructed his editor to fix my bad spelling on the phrase "hissy fit." After John checked it out, he told Tank that it was probably some sort of slang. It is, and my sarcastic sense of humor sometimes still gets me in trouble.

Tank is from Cuba—yes, he is Hispanic. He lived for 13 years under Fidel Castro's Communist regime. When he came to the U.S., he eventually joined the Marine Corps just like his Uncle. Tank is a good man—imperfect, volatile, but has a good heart. He doesn't tolerate betrayal, which is fully understandable. But the main thing is that he absolutely loves America. He knows the importance of what America stands for...and he will fight for her according to the oath he took in the Marines. His daughter is beautiful and I bet she ends up in the Marine Corps or at least in military service.

And there's that Marine thing—don't EVER call a Marine Veteran a "former Marine." First time I did that it...the response was almost frightening. One of the core Marine Corps beliefs is "once a Marine, always a Marine." I did learn my lesson after the initial uproar. Whew. Their culture is unique in the military, but totally awesome.

I asked Tank to write something for the book and he got carried away:

I could literally write a book about my dear friend Faye Higbee, she's is more than a friend, she's is the family member I never had. She's the most loyal, most sweet wholesome person I have ever met in my life and will probably ever will. I sometimes think she's a godsend because many of our successes have been from being always there and helped by pushing us forward. Faye's dedication to the mission at hand, the tens of thousands of hours, the late nights, the working through holidays, seven days a week nonstop is indescribable. No single person outside of me has worked on Uncle Sam's Misguided Children as much as I have except Faye Higbee. I know personally I have driven her crazy more times than I can count and am glad she has the patience, wisdom and understanding to work through it all. Everyone thinks I am the voice of Uncle Sam's Misguided Children, but truthfully the voice is of a conservative God fearing woman whose love for our Military, First responders and America, is above and beyond anyone's capability. Love her more than she will ever know and Uncle Sam's Misguided Children is blessed to have her on our side. Love my friend very much. Tank — Rick Ferran

Yeah, he loves me. And the feeling is mutual.

When I started in 2013, we had a writing stable of about 10 writers. Slowly and sometimes rapidly, they disappeared. Some of them had angst against Tank. Some of them had life happen. Eventually we ended up with a few part-time folks and an occasional guest blogger, but mostly me, the somewhat exhausted "ninja multi-tasker." And then there are people who hate whatever I write. I'll just keep doing my job, no matter what. If the Lord can stand by me through all my ups and downs, I can stand with my friends.

CHAPTER 54

Marines

THE HISTORY OF the Marine Corps is a point of pride — Marines don't just fight for their battle buddies and America, they fight for all who have gone before them. They have a couple of other nicknames: "Leathernecks" (which refers to a solid piece of leather worn around the neck to prevent beheading by the Barbary Pirates), "Teufel Hunden" or Devil Dogs, a name given to them by German Troops from WWI. They were born in a tavern in 1775, and they are proud of it. Don't make a Marine mad, they know how to win battles.

The Facebook page is for Constitutional Conservatives. Many are also veterans who have served our nation in several branches for Army, Navy, Marine Corps, Coast Guard, and Air Force or Reserves/National Guard. Many are First Responders — police, fire, and medical. I have always loved the military, as many of my relatives served. And I am proud of my family's heritage of fighting in the Revolutionary War. It's why America means so much to me.

This part of my life has been a joy, for the most part. I've been able to interview many veterans, and several famous people. In 2015, I was privileged to go to Washington DC twice in one year. The first time was to cover the Blackwater Sentencing (Raven 23) at the U.S. District Court. Being with the wonderful families of the men sentenced was awesome, as they welcomed me with open arms. They have been through deep emotional trauma at being separated from their loved ones. But they work hard to #KeepTheFaith.

The next time was for a special medal ceremony at the Pentagon with Pauline Boyle. Her Marine Veteran husband, Tom, was murdered in Afghanistan while he was a contractor, and was posthumously awarded the Defense of Freedom Medal.

I loved being at the Pentagon, even if the poor tour guides had to walk backwards for a couple of hours while talking to us. Yeah, they really do that. I'd break my neck.

God Bless America, and all of my Misguided friends.

I bet I'd have loved that Tank guy. I hope you're ok with all the work, and I'm glad you have stuck with it. Faithfulness and loyalty seem to be something humans have forgotten or don't care about. I do know that sometimes people can hurt others with their nastiness. Just don't let it ruin your heart.

Yep, that's the truth, Red.

CHAPTER 55

The Ghosts of War

I MET AN ARMY Master Sgt named Tim Shelton over the internet towards the end of his Afghanistan deployment in 2014. We chatted off and on via Facebook, and I was hoping to recruit him to write for our blog. He was excited about coming home to the USA, and even sent me a picture of his men waiting at Bagram airbase to get on the transport home. But when he arrived on US soil, the ghosts of war came with him.

Most people do not understand that PTSD is a physiological response to stress chemicals that have built up inside the brain after multiple traumas. If you're being shot at on a regular basis, and are in a constant state of tension, it can happen. Not everyone gets it, of course. Tim didn't realize that those chemicals had created a problem in his brain. Understand that it is not mental illness... it is a physical response to a stimulus.

Within a few months after Tim returned, he had moved from his home into a camper that only had one door that he could defend. He couldn't sleep. He had counseling from a professional. But counseling cannot remove chemicals that are swimming around in the brain. The counselor tried her best, but it did not work. And pills only mask the problem, they do not fix it.

Then the Army, in its lack of wisdom, decided to medically discharge Tim. He was devastated. They took his only purpose in life and threw it in the dumpster. It was a double whammy: not only did he have difficulties that medical science wasn't able to fix, his Army, his brotherly connection, was broken. After my last communication with him in June of 2015, he took his own life. It left his wife Amy with a major broken heart. It broke the hearts of his men, who deeply loved him and were grateful to have served with him. And it rattled me to the core. You can read about the progression at "Tribute to Brothers Lost" on the Uncle Sam's Misguided Children website.

A few other friends have been lost since 2013, some from suicide, some from medical issues, but the reality is that their lives matter. Their families matter. If you have a veteran or a law enforcement officer in your life, keep in touch with them and encourage them. If you're in close proximity, make an effort to get together to let them know you are a friend. Veterans prefer veterans for friends, but they do appreciate caring.

As of the writing of this book I'm still with my 'misguided' friends. There are many sad stories of abuse by the Veterans Administration, the loss of service members who gave their all for the country, police officers killed in the line of duty… and even the loss of Military or Police Working dogs in the line of duty. I spend some days with tears streaming down my face after interviewing people who have lost sons and daughters, husbands or wives. These are people, even dogs, who have given their lives serving others. Let's support them and never forget their sacrifices.

Thanks for caring. I hear that 20-22 veterans die every day from suicide. Whether it's the problem of not getting good medical care at the VA or just being left alone without their brothers in arms to help them, it's bad on all counts. I'm glad you care about the lives of both humans and animals. Are you ok?

Just a little sad, Red. But I'm ok.

SECTION 9
Cash

CHAPTER 56

Proof that we are Dog-Untrainers

CASH CAME TO live with us after Red passed away from diabetes complications. We found him online from a shelter in Troy, Montana that was about to have to take him in after his owners were moving. Part Labrador retriever and, er, something else, we thought he was a Newfoundland mix. We were wrong. He was not very old when we picked him up, but we noted immediately he was shall we say, rambunctious.

We were used to our dogs sleeping in our bedroom. That went out the window the first night, as he hopped up on the bed and made himself at home, dirt, hair and all. I don't do well at sleeping with a pile of dog hair in my sheets. I know, narrow minded.

The next escapade was when we realized he wasn't a giver. He was a thief. He took my husband's underwear outside and ran around the backyard with them in his mouth. He was trying to play "keep away." We haven't been able to break him of that, so we just lock all our underwear and shoes up. He loves to steal towels, loaves of bread, anything that happens to be on the edge of the counter. Occasionally he gets a mouse. Ugh.

He goes with us on Christmas tree hunts, and a few other excursions. And he does come when called. Most of the time. He loves people. Even gets along with other dogs. We also kill vacuum cleaners around here because of his hair. It's in the food, and coffee, in case you need a little floss.

Photo by Jerry Higbee
Cash, Granddaughter Maddie, and her dog Micah

The people who stay with us and fail to shut their bedroom door pay for it with shoes that become dog toys... chewed up by a dog that we have fully trained to eat anything and be a bad dog. And we're good at it. Bring your dog to our house and we'll have it untrained within 24 hours.

On occasion he'll drag me onto the pavement, or push me out of the car into a parking lot, but I've always lived through it.

All in all, he's a lover dog. He is a good boy, in spite of our ineptness at training. He rules the roost around here. And that's ok. He belongs to us and we wouldn't have it any other way.

Is that defiance? Just asking.

I know you love him. Good thing you have strong bones with falling like that. And you've dealt with dog hair your whole life. Patience is a virtue, you know.

Yes, Red, boy do I know that one. Cash is a dog and I know that well. And he's too smart for his own good.

EPILOGUE
by Red Dog

Faye's life journeys are not much different than other people's journeys, if truth be told. But for everyone, there are choices. How humans handle those choices is the reason she wanted me to help share her life journeys and the lessons they contain.

Her choices in life have been both good and bad. She is imperfect like everyone else, but she has learned to overcome whatever happens by making better choices and not falling backward into emotional swamps that destroy hope. She has learned it through healing in her relationships to God, family and friends. Each experience, each moment, has brought with it fresh horizons. And each step makes a picture of the past, present and future. People can change, and if you get nothing else in these thoughts, that one is a big one.

I hope you will be able to relate to her life and my observations in a way that brings newness to your life journeys.

ABOUT THE AUTHOR

Faye is the author of numerous short stories, newsletters, articles, and blogs. She has won awards for both her writing and her digital photography. She enjoys laughter, and in her words, "I've never claimed to be sane." She lives with her husband Myron in North Idaho, along with her current dog buddy, Cash. She currently writes news articles as the Columnist Manager for Uncle Sam's Misguided Children, a US Marine Veteran-owned website with over 2 million followers. She serves as a board member to three ministries, the board of Bitterroot Mountain Publishing House, and is the Editor of PraiseNet, an international prayer network for A Company of Women International. She is an ordained minister, and pastors Raven Ministries.

You can contact the author at fhigbee@bmphmedia.com.

www.ingramcontent.com/pod-product-compliance
Lightning Source LLC
Chambersburg PA
CBHW060517100426
42743CB00009B/1347